PURPOSE TO PERFORMANCE

PURPOSE

to

PERFORMANCE

*INNOVATIVE
NEW VALUE
CHAINS*

ANDREW GAULE

PURPOSE TO PERFORMANCE

Innovative New Value Chains

ISBN   978-1-61961-653-0 *Hardcover*

978-1-61961-651-6 *Paperback*

978-1-61961-652-3 *Ebook*

LIONCREST
PUBLISHING

*To my wife, Marie, and to my children, Mia and
Ava, who are inspirations for their insights on people,
technology, social media, and the future.*

To the people who see the future and take action to make it better.

CONTENTS

BOOK FOCUS AND CROSS-REFERENCES

This book has been deliberately kept focused on the key strategic story for innovation, corporate venture capital, and Innovative New Value Chains to support organizations having the strategic alignment discussion. To see detailed examples by technology and sector, I have provided access to more than one hundred interviews and videos. There is also an online glossary and many other presentations and resources I am happy to share in order to support organizations on the important journey to helping accelerate the technologies and start-ups that will enhance people and the planet in a profitable approach.

Throughout this book, I will refer to interviews, videos, presentations, and other content. This content is generally referenced by the speaker/author, organization, and date of original publication. Links to the resources are available at aimava.com/resources.

The audience for this book is executive board members who want to understand how technology and new business model development can be facilitated by innovation, venturing, and start-up investment. Executives who develop and lead the innovation and venture programs will find the book invaluable to providing a framework for their strategic relevance. The book will also provide a communication aid for these audiences.

Please feel free to share the cartoons from the book under Creative Commons, not for financial benefit, and attribute to Andrew Gaule (@agaule).

FOREWORD

To produce this book, I have drawn on more than seventeen years' experience working with leading global corporates and interviewing some fantastic, talented, and driven people who are leading innovation and venturing in their organizations. A number have also been generous with their time and have shared their perspectives here to open the book.

Traditionally, companies like PepsiCo and many of our peers were skeptical of ideas that were "not invented here." We've all invested a lot of time, energy, and capital to be best in class in our respective fields. But the pace of change today is such that being the best at current state-of-the-art technologies is no longer enough.

The biggest threat established players face today is someone coming up with a very different business model and changing the game completely—that is, disruptive innovation. That means you have to use every resource available to make sure you're on the edge of that disruption—something you can't do by exploring only within the four walls of your company.

For the past decade, PepsiCo has been actively working to develop the partnerships and internal capabilities that will position us on the path to delivering on our commitment to deliver sustainable growth while leaving a positive imprint on society and the environment.

In *Purpose to Performance: Driving Innovative New Value Chains,* Andrew outlines a path to corporate venturing that helps large corporates ensure they are connected to the new technologies that will be their future growth engines.

—DR. MEHMOOD KHAN
VICE-CHAIRMAN AND CHIEF
SCIENTIFIC OFFICER, PEPSICO

GE Ventures is a catalyst to GE's goal of making the world work better. An innovation engine within GE, our collective of innovators believe unlike forces must converge to grow ideas into technologies that build, cure, move, power, and connect our world of tomorrow. That's why we're located at the intersection of industrial and digital, financial and strategic, time tested and brand new.

Purpose to Performance: Driving Innovative New Value Chains is a testament to Andrew's servant leadership in the corporate venture capital community and offers an important view of the role organizations must play as they face both the opportunities and the challenges of the future. It should be required reading for all corporate innovation leaders!

—SUE SIEGEL
CEO, GE VENTURES

Innovation (i.e., the search for something new and disruptive to existing paradigms and systems) is typically thought of as solely the purview of the start-up company, backyard garage entrepreneur, or the inhabitants of an insulated geography, such as Silicon Valley in California. Rarely, if ever, does one think about innovation being found, much less thriving in a large, corporate, bureaucratic setting.

However, to survive and excel in today's marketplace, established players and corporates are required to think differently and find new ideas in unusual places. Enter the world of corporate venture capital and innovation, where a mutually beneficial relationship between new and established corporates and ecosystems can thrive.

Through his visionary leadership and vast network, Andrew Gaule has worked tirelessly to organize and highlight the best practices of corporate venture capital enabling this reinvigorated industry to grow and flourish. When we began to explore ways to bring cutting-edge technologies and solutions into our organization in order to better serve our members and customers, one of the first places I turned to was Andrew's organization to better understand the intricacies and nuances of corporate venture in order to best position our efforts internally to create successfully leverage and scale this new effort. Without Andrew and the global corporate venture community he has marshaled together, I don't think we would have been successful in standing up our strategic innovation portfolio, much less putting it in the best position to succeed going forward.

—ERIC L. STEAGER
DIRECTOR, CORPORATE DEVELOPMENT &
INNOVATION, INDEPENDENCE BLUE CROSS
MANAGING DIRECTOR, STRATEGIC
INNOVATION PORTFOLIO

The pace and scope of innovation is accelerating within society as technologies and business models are coming together to disrupt all major corporates around the globe. I have worked in IBM for thirty years in senior R&D roles, and I led the ventures initiative.

I have seen the rise and transformation of corporate venturing and have developed a more effective engagement model for IBM to work with the venture ecosystem. For me, the approach to innovation is to bring together the "string of pearls" of technology and start-ups. Andrew has been key in developing and implementing what he has termed Innovative New Value Chain, which is driving more strategic corporate venturing and change.

This book brings together the leading thinking Andrew delivers in his accredited Corporate Venturing Academy and his years of experience in helping corporates drive their strategic innovation. Andrew has also been a great advocate for diversity of gender, race, and age, while working globally to make corporates, the innovation ecosystem, and society better.

—CLAUDIA FAN MUNCE, RETIRED FOUNDER
OF IBM VENTURE CAPITAL GROUP
CURRENTLY VENTURE ADVISER AT NEA
(ONE OF THE WORLD'S LARGEST AND MOST
ACTIVE VENTURE CAPITAL FIRMS)

Having set up Martlet, the corporate venturing arm of Marshall of Cambridge, a £2 billion revenue, 100-plus-year-old aerospace and engineering company, six years ago and personally having been a superactive (55+ investments) technology angel for the last decade,

I have watched many large companies investigate, set up, and run corporate ventures.

The primary issue for senior executives is to understand their company's policy on financial (i.e., does one hope for a positive return) versus strategic (i.e., how does one "value" the soft elements) returns from corporate investments (as opposed to M&A transactions) now and as the company evolves.

A secondary issue to consider is how to resource the initiative in terms of staffing and capital to be deployed, bearing in mind that investments will be illiquid for an indeterminate period (the capital will need to be patient), and skills may need to be brought in from outside the company.

Third, a system needs to be put into place to ensure dissemination of technology and other knowledge from the investee company around the corporate.

—PETER COWLEY
CAMBRIDGE-BASED SERIAL TECH ENTREPRENEUR
AND ANGEL INVESTOR, CHARITY CHAIR AND TRUSTEE,
MENTOR, AND NONEXECUTIVE DIRECTOR. NAMED
UK BUSINESS ANGEL OF THE YEAR 2014/15 AND BEST
ANGEL OF THE WORLD BY THE WORLD BUSINESS
ANGEL INVESTMENT FORUM IN FEBRUARY 2017

For every business, it is important to keep its portfolio up to date through introducing new technologies and business models. For that, a good strategic overview externally and internally is needed, plus the openness to collaborate. For many years, Andrew Gaule has consistently helped to connect entrepreneurial people, providing invaluable insights into ways to leverage new forms of innovation.

—ROB VAN LEEN
CHIEF INNOVATION OFFICER
MEMBER EXECUTIVE COMMITTEE
DSM

We live in a world where the pace of technology and change is accelerating at an ever-increasing rate. Many industries are being fundamentally disrupted by digitization, and this poses both great opportunities and great threats to established players who fail to adapt.

I passionately believe we need to work to bring together new ideas, innovative start-ups, corporates, and investors to drive a coherent and joined-up approach to the adoption and implementation of solutions and products, for the benefit of society.

I have known Andrew, through his work in the corporate venturing community, for many years. His work in breaking down silos in corporate thinking and in disseminating best practice to assist in opening up opportunities through corporate venturing and open innovation has been of immense value to the community. I am convinced this new book will help to stimulate new thinking and to disseminate the great work he has been doing.

—HAZEL MOORE OBE
COFOUNDER AND CHAIRMAN, FIRSTCAPITAL
MEMBER OF THE BOARD, INNOVATEUK

The Industrial Revolution was built around the intellectual property of Watt, Tesla, Westinghouse, and many others. But today, many CEOs and C-suite executives miss the relevance of intellectual property (IP), which underpins 70 to 80 percent of the value of most companies. Whether it's formal IP in the shape of patents or trademarks, or simply intellectual assets such as trade secrets (that need to be kept secret), integrating all this into the overall company strategy is essential to success.

And for those who think saying China and IP in the same breath is an oxymoron—think again. China is well on its way to having one of the world's best IP systems; it's creating more formal IP than the next twenty countries combined, and, quite soon, that IP will be leading edge and truly innovative on a massive scale. China is a country, market, and source of business ideas that you ignore at your long-term peril.

Linking larger corporates with the smaller, innovative companies that are generating the new technologies and products is difficult to do well, but Andrew brings together the many strands that today are necessary for success.

—IAN HARVEY

CEO, BTG (1985–2004)

CHAIRMAN, IP CENTER ADVISORY BOARD,

TSINGHUA UNIVERSITY X-LAB, BEIJING

ADJUNCT PROFESSOR, IMPERIAL COLLEGE

BUSINESS SCHOOL, LONDON, AND MEMBER

OF ITS IP CENTRE ADVISORY BOARD

ADVISER TO AIMAVA

For more than seventeen years, we have been investing in technologies and markets that are strategically important for RELX's businesses. Over this time, RELX has been one of the few print-based information providers to successfully transform its business and operations to become a market-leading online information, data, and analytics company.

At REV Venture Partners—a global venture capital partnership with a single limited partner, RELX

Group—our belief is that every industry is becoming an information industry. Our areas of focus include software as a service (SaaS)/Ourcloud, data and analytics, machine learning, artificial intelligence, and next-generation technologies such as blockchain—all of which are important trends for RELX business units.

Our team is based in London, but we invest internationally with more than 80 percent of our portfolio based in the United States, predominantly in Silicon Valley. We spend most of our time in profiling markets of interest, originating investment opportunities from our networks, negotiating and closing financing rounds, and sitting on boards and supporting our portfolio companies. Importantly, we also spend roughly 30 percent of our time working with RELX business units. Our investment activity, which involves reviewing thousands of early-stage companies a year, enables us to provide a complementary lens on the evolution of RELX business segments and interpret the impact of medium- and long-term technology trends on their businesses.

In this book and in his academy, Andrew plays an important role in building the capability and strategic understanding of senior executives on the best corporate venture capital and business approaches.

I am pleased to have worked with Andrew over many years and have seen him in action helping businesses build capabilities for effective strategic and operational alignment of venturing and business units.

—TONY ASKEW
FOUNDER PARTNER, REV VENTURE PARTNERS
CHAIR, BRITISH VENTURE CAPITAL
ASSOCIATION (BVCA) VC GROUP

INTRODUCTION
GRASPING THE TECHNOLOGY AND INNOVATION OPPORTUNITIES

Do feel free to share!
@agaule

Technology has reached a previously unknown level of maturity and availability, greatly altering how modern businesses grow and perform. We have seen the phenomenal rise of companies such as Google, Uber, Tencent, Tesla, and Huawei. Thanks to disruptive innovation, the speed of change is so great that a "business as usual" approach no longer works for today's leading companies.

As technologies converge and create business models that are spurring competition from different sectors, it is not sufficient to innovate in a current industry.

In this book, we will go on a journey of the changing technology and how organizations need to align their strategy and processes to deliver strategic and financial returns. I will explain the strategic importance of innovation and effective corporate venturing, as I believe there is a need to go beyond just innovating and investing.

Looking outside the organization is key to see new technology and business models that were "not invented here." Organizations now need to be joining start-ups, technologies, and corporates to create new business models globally. This is what we have termed Innovative New Value Chains®, and building them will improve people's lives and the planet as we tackle the challenges in health, food, transport, urban living, and many other areas.

Embracing Innovative New Value Chains means companies must first define their strategic objectives, search the markets, and subsequently invest in ways that allow them to look beyond existing business models to drive long-term growth.

There are organizations leading the way. There will be many examples in this book, and many more in the resources, giving insights to the changes in the organizations and industries.

- **Merck**, a health company, has a Global Health Innovation Fund led by William (Bill) Taranto with a focus on digital health. In an interview with me, Taranto said, "You have to build a strategy around how you are going to invest and how you are actually going to scale, and then bring that value back to your parent company."

- **RELX** (formerly called Reed Elsevier) has moved from paper-based information publishing to decision support systems and is a world-leading provider of information and analytics for professional and business customers across industries.

- **DSM** has transformed itself, moving from coal mining in Holland to health, nutrition, and materials.

- **BP Venturing** plays a key role in BP corporate strategy by helping the transition to a low-carbon energy future, leveraging its investments across a wide portfolio of relevant technology businesses.

- **GE** is moving, on an industrial scale, toward being a "software" company, as data will be the core of future business.

- **Unilever** has been innovating and venturing for more than fifteen years in sustainability, personal care, and digital marketing, which has brought financial and strategic returns.

- **IBM** is continuing the transition from a computer hardware company to cloud platform and cognitive solutions company—the basis of many of the new technologies behind the start-ups and corporates going through the change.

These companies know that the path to big-picture growth involves more than modifying the current suite of products in their respective industries or making ad hoc investments. Instead, those businesses continue to harness the power of disruptive innovation, gathering knowledge, investing, and acquiring to create new business models. They are delivering valuable strategic insight and new business areas for the core business. Also, we will see that one of them has created a billion-dollar entity with its corporate venture capital and private equity transaction.

THE VALUE OF STRATEGIZING FOR CHANGE

The convergence of technology creates both opportunities and disruption to leading corporates. A business that ignores such innovation risks a "Kodak moment"—that is, the possibility of going, like Kodak, into liquidation in just a few years as it fails to meet the fundamental change in its industry.

Most organizations do not face the threat of this kind of rapid obsolescence, but they could very well miss multibillion-dollar opportunities caused by their failure to adapt to the changing digital marketplace. Incumbent corporates might have the right technologies, a standout relationship with customers, multiple distribution channels, and a brand they can leverage into a new disruptive industry by way of Innovative New Value Chains.

DEVELOPING A STRATEGIC INNOVATION STRATEGY

Having stakeholders and executives *say* they are going to innovate is not enough to produce real results, even at the incremental level. For many executives, proactively facing disruptive innovation means understanding the scale of the issue, balancing the various innovations, and joining up the delivery. For this process to be effective, there must be a clear method to guide the way. We are going to go through the 5Ps of Innovation and Venturing, which have been effectively used for more than ten years in leading corporates to address the key challenges and questions organizations face:

- *Purpose.* What is the purpose of the innovations the business is trying to address? Incremental innovation to improve the current business is a valid answer, but disruptive innovation is a different matter entirely, bringing different technology and business models together. Defining the purpose of the endeavor is a critical first step.

- *Process.* What will the innovation process look like for this particular business? Different "purpose" objectives will drive different processes. We will cover the range of processes from fund investing, to direct investment, incubation, partnering, and so forth.

- *People.* People are central to the 5Ps. Are the right types of people looking outside the organization effectively, building strategic narratives with executives, and driving a process involving start-up investments?

- *Partners.* Have the right partners, outside the scope of the organization's current capabilities, been selected?

- *Performance.* What is the appropriate balance of short-term financial return and strategic, long-term growth, and how can organizations measure this?

The 5Ps is an iterative process. Purpose, process, partners, and performance all circle around a center: people. The method was built on the concept of adapting and learning, a cycle focused on moving forward in the face of fundamental change to build a winning strategic innovation and building Innovative New Value Chains.

Investing today is not enough; it is strategically important to gather data to create new business models that result in strategic innovation and change. Currently, corporates are not joining the pieces together properly—that is where Innovative New Value Chains come into play. The purpose of this book is to enhance the discussion between innovation areas in the business and give a framework for discussion with C-suite executives and boards.

This book's first chapter will explain the fundamentals of corporate venturing. Subsequent chapters will explore each component of the 5Ps and provide additional information, including basic legal considerations for corporate venturing, overviews of the leading global innovation superpowers in the space, and techniques for leveraging analytics to drive optimal growth. This discussion ultimately leads to a thorough examination of Innovative New Value Chains strategy. Having developed the 5Ps method in the early 2000s, I set out to build a framework to help businesses struggling with innovation launch strategic discussions. I first published the 5Ps method in my

2006 book *Open Innovation in Action: How to Be Strategic in the Search for New Sources of Value*, and I have more than seventeen years' experience helping corporates reach their corporate venturing goals, which can now be truly strategic.

1. UNDERSTANDING THE FUNDAMENTALS OF STRATEGIC INNOVATION AND CORPORATE VENTURING

Do feel free to share!
@agaule

A key approach in open innovation for exploring technology and business models outside the organization is corporate venturing. Corporate venturing describes partnering with start-ups outside your organization and often investing in a minority stake—that is, making an investment for usually less than 20 percent of the equity or stock. Understanding the fundamentals of corporate venturing starts with examining a snapshot of how it looks in today's leading global companies.

With data from GCV Analytics, we will see in more detail in the data chapter (chapter ten) that 1,667 corporate investors have been tracked from 2011 to 2016, with 965 making a deal in 2016.[1]

Examples from some of the largest and most dynamic corporates, such as Intel, and the rising big funds of Alibaba and Tencent from China, will be considered. Also covered will be innovation and funds in sectors of health, oil, consumer goods, financials, and more. In chapter nine, I will outline how these sectors are likely to become more strategic as we see the rise of China as an economic superpower.

The rise in the number of investments, along with the broader partnering and open innovation, is a testament to the organizations' recognition of the value of looking outside. In the foreword, Mehmood Khan, vice-chairman and chief scientific officer of PepsiCo, explained, "You have to use every resource available to make sure you're on the edge of that disruption—something you can't do by exploring only within the four walls of your company." As my letter in the *Financial Times*[2] stated, "Thinking in

---

1   James Mawson, *World of Corporate Venturing 2017* (report, Mawsonia, 2017).

2   Andrew Gaule, "Don't Get Boxed In—Embrace People with 'Extrepreneurial' Skills," *Financial Times*, July 29, 2005, http://www.ft.com/cms/s/0/cb948562-ffcd-11d9-86df-00000e2511c8.html?ft_site=falcon&desktop=true#axzz4o5aPOE4O.

other people's boxes is more productive than an internal workshop that tries to think outside the box."

THE WORLD OF CORPORATE VENTURING

Corporates can become involved in corporate venturing as executives start in a division or function doing direct investments. The alternative is a top-down approach driven by a high degree of strategy. Whichever way an organization enters the world of corporate venturing, the key players must come together to define and meet a strategic objective.

Different corporates approach venturing differently. For example, corporates can invest as limited partners (LPs) in external funds. Or they can choose to operate from a general partner and limited partner (GP/LP) fund in which the venturing business is a separate legal entity and the corporate is a limited partner investor within the fund. (Find greater detail of these and other terms in the glossary, located in the Sources of Further Information section of the book.[3]) Other companies make investments from their own budgets—that is, off-balance-sheet investments. Businesses can forgo investments in favor of partnering with start-ups to provide new capabilities that spur mutually beneficial growth and innovation. We will

---

3   Find a glossary containing these and other terms at Aimava.com/resources.

see examples of these different approaches in the process and partner chapters.

We will see examples of corporate venture units such as Merck, DSM, Unilever, BP, Intel, and Tencent that are making financially rewarding investments and providing important strategic value to the parent corporate.

THE STATE OF CORPORATE VENTURING TODAY

Identifying a new technology poised to disrupt an industry and taking minority-stake investments in a start-up within that space is typically termed corporate venture capital (CVC). It often takes seven to fifteen years for a company following this path to see financial return, as that is how long it takes technology and start-up to go through their growth phases, ultimately exiting through a trade sale, stock market flotation, or a liquidation. Some executives expect results within two to three years and shut down the corporate venturing unit when those returns do not materialize as quickly as they would like. Organizations should expect to evolve their programs so they sustain their innovation by retaining the people who have built up the knowledge and the networks.

Searching for the next big thing in technology is hard for a corporation, and many technologies—smart mobile devices, big data, cloud computing, new materials—while growing, still have room to be applied more effectively. The corporate venturing units and strategic innovation teams in a corporate need to consider application of the technology, as much as finding the technology itself.

Start-ups and incubators—organizations that support and nurture start-ups—appear to help bridge this efficiency gap, but that impression is clouded over by another issue: saturation. According to the UK-published report "Business Incubators and Accelerators: The National Picture,"[4] there are 205 incubators and 163 accelerators—support systems for young start-ups—currently active in the United Kingdom, and these together support more than 7,000 businesses each year. These are largely funded by corporates. This situation creates stacks of start-ups, and corporates tend to invest in their technologies for technology's sake—an approach not only lacking in strategy but also unlikely to produce positive returns.

Another problem for modern corporate venturing units is the frequent lack of information sharing between groups within organizations. I have seen many instances of R&D not discussing with Finance, Strategy, and Marketing

---

4   Jonathan Bone, Olivia Allen, and Christopher Haley, "Business Incubators and Accelerators: The National Picture" (Department of Business, Energy & Industrial Strategy, 2017).

when they have different responsibilities for further out innovation. If the corporate venturing unit and C-suite are not communicating, for example, it is nearly impossible for the company vision to respond to new opportunities.

Sometimes a corporate venturing unit following the afore-mentioned approach *will* succeed in making returns. Along the way, though, it risks missing important opportunities outside its core business, leading to long-term losses in innovation potential and future profits.

A BETTER APPROACH

An effective corporate venturing approach is one in which the corporate venturing unit is operated like a traditional venture capital organization. The venturing unit might look at between five hundred and one thousand oppor-tunities and do due diligence—detailed financial, market, business, and people research—on between fifty and one hundred of them. In the end, that well-run corporate ven-turing unit will invest in three to six of those opportunities. All the while, the corporate venturing unit will provide insight to the executives and business units, which will then offer feedback on when the organization should move into such new opportunities.

Reviewing so many opportunities creates a funnel that

allows company stakeholders to get a view of the ways in which technologies are changing and could potentially disrupt business models across industries. This perspective is a key component of creating successful strategic innovation and Innovative New Value Chains through corporate venturing. In these instances, the financial return from corporate venturing is important for the sustainability of the unit and is strategically important, with insight and relationships gained from the endeavor.

THE FOUR STAGES OF INNOVATION MATURITY

Thanks to the influx of technology and associated opportunities into the market, an innovation strategy is critical to a business's longevity. Corporates generally fall into one of the following stages along the Maturity Curve for Innovation:

- **Stage Zero: No Innovation Strategy**. If executives in an organization have absolutely no awareness of the need to innovate to remain competitive, that business falls under Stage Zero.

- **Stage One: Initial Innovation Strategy.** A corporation in Stage One recognizes the need to innovate, yet remains passive. Although executives understand their industry might be disrupted by better understandings of consumer needs, megatrends, new technologies, and new players, they take little action.

- **Stage Two: Active Innovation Strategy.** If a corporation is in Stage Two, it has recognized the value of integrating innovation into its business model and created a forward-thinking plan of action born out of that recognition. Most corporates now participating in open innovation and corporate venturing, running incubators, investing in start-ups, and so forth, fall into this category. Although they are undoubtedly making progress, they are not yet integrating a significant strategic approach.

- **Stage Three: Innovative New Value Chains.** A corporation in Stage Three has reached a mature innovation, connecting the dots to develop new business models and extract new value. It has put start-ups and new technologies to work, while creating new methods for delivering products and services.

Some call this phase Corporate Venturing 3.0. In my opinion, this is not a good term, as it still focuses on corporate venturing's transactional processes rather than its strategic and business impact. *Ecosystem investing* is a term that may also be used, but this misses the proactive aspect of putting new tech and business models into action.

The benefits come from creating larger-scale opportunities that will be strategic for the corporate and likely to have better financial returns.

Executives in Stage Zero will have never picked up this book, as they have not recognized the critical role of innovation in their industry and business model. Most modern organizations fall under Stage One or Stage Two. The many companies used as positive examples in this book are either well on the journey to Stage Three or already there.

THE RELATIONSHIP BETWEEN CORPORATE VENTURING AND INNOVATION

There are many corporate venturing techniques: participating in corporate partnering, joining together with universities, investing directly, investing in funds, acting as an incubator, and so on. While the processes are different, they all have one thing in common: their success hinges on innovation, long-term vision, and healthy communication between the C-suite and corporate venturing managers. Accomplishing this goal means breaking down silos, repairing broken reporting processes, and sharing insights with key players.

Royal DSM is a global science-based company active

in health, nutrition, and materials. DSM was formed in 1902 by the Dutch government to mine coal in the southern province of the Netherlands and was known as Dutch State Mines. It was diversifying until it closed its last mine in 1973. Looking to innovation as a solution to expand the business, DSM embraced discontinuity in a way that created a breadth of new potential markets and products. Thanks to a robust open innovation and corporate venturing with access to the C-suite and direction from Chief Innovation Officer (CIO) Rob Van Leen,[5] the entire business model has continued to shift from mining to producing bulk chemicals, specialty chemicals, and biomaterials. In the case of DSM and companies like it, the *right* people with the *right* access and governance led to the creation of the *right* innovations, fundamentally transforming the business so it could thrive in the modern world.

THE 5PS: PATH TO INNOVATION AND CV MATURITY

Stage Three on the Maturity of Innovation is where a business needs to be to most benefit from its corporate venturing and innovation initiatives. Organizations need to achieve alignment of the strategic innovation and venturing. I term this the 5Ps, and organizations need to explore the approach, taking into consideration their

---

5   Rob van Leen, DSM, May 2017 and Apr. 2012—Podcast Interviews.

industry, their organization, and the disruption that technology and new business models will cause for them (see figure 1).

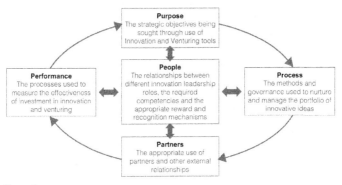

Purpose
The strategic objectives being sought through use of Innovation and Venturing tools

Performance
The processes used to measure the effectiveness of investment in innovation and venturing

People
The relationships between different innovation leadership roles, the required competencies and the appropriate reward and recognition mechanisms

Process
The methods and governance used to nurture and manage the portfolio of innovative ideas

Partners
The appropriate use of partners and other external relationships

Figure 1

For more than ten years, the 5Ps has been used as an effective method by hundreds of executives to develop their effective strategic innovation. An important distinction must be drawn here: While the 5Ps method leads to more strategic innovation and an effective basis to develop Innovative New Value Chains, that does not negate the benefit of incremental innovation. The light bulb was not invented from incrementally improving the candle. The light bulb, however, *has* seen significant incremental improvements—smarter light bulbs, lower-energy light bulbs—that have been important to the industry, offering improvements in both cost, efficiency, and more functionality.

Whether the type of innovation a company is pursuing is incremental or big picture, success along the journey is contingent on understanding the fundamentals of corporate venturing. It also hinges on how well a business moves through the 5Ps—a process that starts by identifying purpose, which is explored in chapter two. Processes across a spectrum of different solutions for stimulating innovation are outlined in chapter three. People—the center of the iterative process—is covered in chapter four. Chapters five and six focus on building relationships with partners and performance measuring the effectiveness of investments, respectively. The culmination of the 5Ps leads to Innovative New Value Chain strategy, explored in chapter seven. Legal considerations are outlined in chapter eight, and an explanation of the value of locating the global innovation superpowers follows in chapter nine. Finally, chapter ten includes a discussion of how to use analytics to drive corporate venturing. At the end of this book, you will find access to more than one hundred interviews in podcasts and videos and additional resources for further reading and listening. This will help you develop the narrative and approach that is appropriate for your organization.

2. PURPOSE: SETTING STRATEGIC OBJECTIVES

Do feel free to share!
@agaule

All parts of the 5Ps method are interrelated, and the initial step is establishing a clear purpose. In this phase, a company clarifies the strategic objectives it seeks as it approaches innovation and corporate venturing. It must also consider the company vision and the need for that vision to be flexible as new technologies, opportunities, and even business models take shape.

THE BENEFITS OF DEFINING PURPOSE

The purpose of innovating is to enable organizations to grow in a way that is sustainable in the long term while providing outcomes that benefit the business, people, and planet along the way. Currently, too many executives are too focused on what I term incremental innovation—short-term focus instead of what will be strategically beneficial over time. Avoiding this trap begins with defining purpose.

There are many key benefits of defining purpose as the first step in the 5Ps:

- **Gaining strategic insights.** As technologies change, so do companies and business models. This allows organizations to align strategy and purpose in areas of the business rooted in change. These strategic insights can help businesses better define the strategic direction of the business for areas in which to develop acquisitions and disposals.

- **Finding new business opportunities.** As technology changes and entire industries are disrupted, business growth opportunities arise in new areas: this is the central theme of the creation of Innovative New Value Chains.

- **Making financial returns.** Investing in successful

businesses in expanding sectors leads to financial returns on investment and, in the parent organization, can lead to new revenue and reduced costs of operations.

THREE HORIZONS OF PURPOSE

Many organizations define their purpose too broadly. For example, saying the purpose is "to be more innovative and grow" lacks the specificity needed to make those words materialize into actions and strategies. In their book *The Alchemy of Growth: Practical Insights for Building the Enduring Enterprise*, Mehrdad Baghai, Stephen Coley, and David White highlight three "horizons" to help businesses meet this challenge:

- **Horizon One: Defend.** Have a focus on defending the core business, endeavoring to improve on current portfolios, bolstering sales strategies, and rationalizing internal costs. Horizon One is all about looking for ways to compete more effectively with a "business as usual" approach.

- **Horizon Two: Grow.** Aim to build on the core business to diversify and free up internal resources, a classic manifestation of growth into adjacencies. For example, an organization looking to apply new technologies to current markets—or to apply existing products to new markets or with new types of customers—falls within Horizon Two.

- **Horizon Three: Explore.** Build scenarios in technologies and markets, creating opportunities through ventures. It is in this horizon that businesses need to explore, turning innovative new business models into growth opportunities either within or adjacent to the core business.

Each horizon contains a viable business strategy. Horizons One and Two help corporates in the short term, yet many executives are not venturing into Horizon Three because they feel it is risky. In fact, *not* paying attention to Horizon Three is the real risk, as I outlined in my 2006 book, *Open Innovation in Action*, because organizations stand to miss the future opportunities or threats coming from technology, new business models, and growing start-ups.

MEGATRENDS LEAD TO FOCUS AREAS

There are significant megatrends that are impacting all organizations, industries, and societies.

- Which megatrends are impacting your organization?

- Demographic

- Technology

- Biotech, special materials

- Mobility

- Energy

- Natural resources, such as water

- Health and wellness

- High-growth regions and shifting economic power

- Urbanization

- New business models

Just a few of the corporates that have presented at programs I have led at Corporate Venturing Academies have highlighted these focus themes:

Evonik,[6] a leading chemicals company, focuses on the following:

6   Corporate Venturing Academy, Warsaw, June 2017.

- Health and nutrition

- Resource efficiency

- Globalization

The above then drives the following growth fields for Evonik:

- Sustainable nutrition

- Advanced food ingredients

- Health-care solutions

- Cosmetic solutions

- Membranes

- Smart materials

Intel Capital,[7] known for accelerating technology change and connectivity, is driving the following focus areas:

- Mobile client and communications

---

7 Corporate Venturing Academy, Warsaw, June 2017.

- Software and security

- New technologies, wearables, and robotics

- Diversity inclusion

- Augmented reality, virtual reality, and cognitive computing

- Sport and health

- Cloud and storage

BP presented on the following venturing areas:

- Advanced mobility

- Bioproducts and low-carbon products

- Carbon management

- Digital transformation

- Power and storage

With just three examples from different industries, we can see common megatrends that are impacting them all.

Listening to the range of interviews and seeing the websites and statements from other organizations, you will see common themes. The strategic focus areas for corporates are not static. And, as areas move to become core business, priorities change or they are judged no longer of value. Unilever Ventures, for example, has had changes of emphasis over the years, with a growing emphasis on sustainability and a move to digital marketing of personal care products and services. As we will see later, it is important to maintain knowledge and partnerships as their areas change. If you do not evolve but just abandon investments, your personal and organizational reputation will be damaged, and you will not be credible in the new strategic area of focus.

MOVING THROUGH THE PURPOSE PHASE

We have seen examples of specific organizations balancing the Three Horizons of Purpose; it is also helpful to examine the evolution of entire industries—the utility business, for example. Companies in Horizon One focus on generating energy: coal, oil, gas, nuclear, and so on. Disruption is occurring for businesses in Horizon Two, as more efficient devices and less environmentally damaging means of generating energy become more commonplace. A Horizon Two focus, for example, may have business models centered on solar panels or wind farming—large contemporary industrial installations.

Horizon Three in the utility industry takes an even more progressive spin on the innovation happening in Horizon Two. Solar panels in homes have led to entire distributed-energy generation and storage systems that can, in turn, be applied in ways that blur lines between industries. The solar-powered battery packs and Tesla vehicles created by Elon Musk, for example, are products of Horizon Three purposeful innovation in the utility industry. The thinking behind Musk's distributed energy management solution is different from that of a traditional utility business, and his application of the technology in vehicles is radically different from that of a traditional car manufacturer. It is great to reflect on a visit I led to Tesla in 2008 with executives from BAE, BOC, Linde, Philips, P&G, and Unilever when the first production car was produced. Today, Tesla's market capitalization has reached the levels of Ford or General Motors (based on future potential), while Tesla car volumes and sales are a small fraction of the two megacorporates.

Musk's success as an innovator represents what happens when a visionary leader has a defined strategic purpose. The result is the *integration* of solutions for mobility, energy storage, and clean generation—what I would term Innovative New Value Chains—that evolve as a business uses new technologies and business models that are outside traditional industry definitions.

DIFFERENT INDUSTRIES, DIFFERENT TIME LINES

Different industries have different time lines for change. The automotive and energy industries, for example, have lengthier product-development cycles and investment cycles than the technology industry or consumer industry. For example, in the oil industry, upstream oil and gas extraction requires long testing and investment cycles that are also critical for safety. Downstream consumer sales and customer interaction tend to have shorter development cycles with lower investment costs.

Now, consider the retail industry: companies investing in brick-and-mortar locations clearly do so because their executives believe that business model will have longevity. Thanks to distributed retail systems, and digital and mobile devices redefining customer experiences, though, the potential for disruption in this industry is tremendous—and it is happening quickly. This is seen more starkly in rapidly developing economies such as China, with the rapid growth of online commerce platforms such as Alibaba and WeChat. We also see that new consumers and younger generations are engaging with retail purchases via social media and delivery services. It will be interesting to see the convergence of online and offline, with acquisitions of the likes of Whole Foods by Amazon, a move announced in June 2017.

"White collar" and knowledge-intensive sectors such as legal, accounting, and medicine are now being affected by technology changes such as artificial intelligence, big data, blockchain, and the Internet of Things (IoT)—all of which contribute to providing automated and powerful knowledge systems.

REDEFINING PURPOSE

Defining purpose is an essential first step on the path to excelling at corporate venturing and ultimately creating new value. Let's examine organizations that repurposed in the face of major industry disruption.

IBM

International Business Machines (IBM) has excelled at repurposing. Initially steeped in computer hardware such as mainframes and PCs, executives realized the old business model was not sustainable in the long term. In 2005, IBM divested its PC business to the Chinese company Lenovo, which is now one of the world's largest PC and mobile devices businesses, along with HP and Dell.

IBM is no longer a computer business: It is a *computing-power* business, described as a global cloud platform and cognitive-solution business, focused on cloud sharing, big data, and providing backend capabilities for the likes of artificial intelligence poster child IBM Watson. IBM provides large and small enterprises the computing power and cognitive abilities they need to exist in the digital marketplace. The business has also transformed into an open-source rather than a proprietary system, further adding value and capabilities for consumers.

IBM had the equivalent of a business near-death experience, emerged, and is now developing new areas. In an industry changing as rapidly as technology, IBM has proved itself to be an organization committed to innovating and challenging parameters. An important part of its success in redefining purpose has come from IBM Ventures, the company's corporate venturing unit, which continually looks for new venturing and partnering opportunities. Wendy Lung[8] and Claudia Fan Munce[9] have described the IBM model for partnering and investing in two of my interviews.

GE

GE Chief Executive Jeff Immelt has been driving the business into the digital arena. Immelt and his team do not just focus on creating engines and industrial systems;

8   Wendy Lung, IBM, Apr. 2011—Podcast Interview.

9   Claudia Fan Munce, IBM, May 2015—Video Interview.

rather, they create the digital platforms to ensure those devices are managed and operated effectively. GE also takes steps to ensure the data generated from these efforts is used optimally to improve processes and outcomes for businesses and consumers, as Immelt described in the CEO letter in the GE 2016 results:

> *We are investing in disruptive innovation that will drive industrial productivity in the future. We have established two new businesses—GE Digital and GE Additive Manufacturing—that are in the early stages of value creation for GE investors.*

Part of this effort is spurred by GE Ventures, the organization's corporate venturing arm. GE Ventures drives change and investments in the health and industrial areas, considering new processes, connected devices, and how the IoT is changing business models around and within operations adjacent to GE. Sue Siegel,[10] in her interview with me in 2014, powerfully discussed strategic purpose being driven by company leadership and manifested through GE Ventures activities. In the following short description, Siegel certainly illustrates the potential to connect new technologies and start-ups globally to solve customer problems and major world issues:

---

10 Sue Siegel, GE Ventures, Jun. 2014—Podcast Interview.

GE Ventures works on identifying, scaling, and accelerating start-ups in the areas of industrial Internet software, advanced manufacturing, energy, and health care. These are clearly areas where the world is facing big challenges. GE Ventures helps entrepreneurs and start-ups succeed by providing access to GE's technical expertise, capital, and opportunities for commercialization through GE's global network of businesses, customers, and partners. We also act as Sherpas to help entrepreneurs access the great level of resources through our Global Research Center, including 35,000 engineers, 5,000 research scientists, 8,000 software professionals, as well as 40,000 sales, marketing, and development resources in over 100 countries.

KEY MESSAGES

Organizations need clarity on their purpose across the Three Horizons, from incremental innovation to disruptive. New technology, start-ups, and business models are going to impact all sectors but perhaps at different paces. The more disruptive changes are going to be outside the current capabilities of an organization and the current industry incumbents.

To determine your organization's purpose, you need to balance innovation and delivery across the Three Horizons. You will need to be doing something outside your current business and different from the current industry and technology models.

PURPOSE TO PERFORMANCE · 57

3. PROCESS: USING THE APPROPRIATE PROCESS TO ACHIEVE YOUR OBJECTIVE

Process follows purpose in the examination of the 5Ps of strategic innovation and corporate venturing. Process describes the approaches to delivering innovation and the methods and governance used to nurture and manage portfolios of innovative ideas. There are a variety of approaches that fall under the umbrella of process; we will cover a range of them in this chapter. It is also important to understand that this involves more than just making an investment, as you need the broader strategic agenda, venture growth, and ability to integrate or change the current business.

Organizations need to use the appropriate process for their purpose. If an organization in the standard manufactured consumer goods sector determines its purpose is to address the challenge to its business from new electronic devices bringing new features such as IoT connectivity, it is not likely to have the right capabilities or people. The business, then, should possibly be investigating and investing in Silicon Valley or Shenzhen.

To caricature the ineffective approach, you do not want a CEO coming back from an event such as Davos, saying they want to be innovative, and then starting the innovation process with a suggestion scheme. It is best if the right process is aligned to a clear purpose from the beginning.

To explore this topic further, consider figure 2—a breakdown of process evolution that can be widely applied. In the graphic, the vertical axis describes purpose, with the bottom left falling into Horizon One and the top left registering as Horizon Three activity. Recall that Horizon One activity means staying closer to core business functions, while Horizon Three activity is radically different from the core business. The use of language is important for many organizations, and using terms such as *disruptive innovation*, *radical*, *Horizon Three*, and *legacy business* will have implications on how the activities are perceived—hence my labeling of "Innovation Ambition."

In figure 2, the horizontal axis holds various types of processes. Core business improvement falls on one end of the spectrum, while corporate venturing—made up of direct investment, indirect venture capital (VC) fund with investment decision input, and indirect VC fund innovation—is on the other. The definitions of some processes and where they are in the spectrum vary by industry and technology.

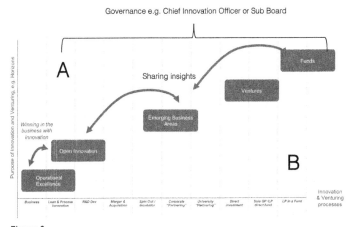

Figure 2

Organizations looking to innovate further from their current business and tapping into technology that is unknown to them are more likely to look further out from their core business and into organizations that are investing in newer technology and business models. Examples of processes are fund investments and direct investment in more radical technology and start-ups. Insights, then, need to come closer to the business to trial and build what some organizations term emerging business areas (EBAs). DSM, for example, has EBAs that include DSM Biomedical, focused on innovative materials for medical devices; DSM Bio-based Products and Services, focused on clean energy from crop residues as well as biochemicals with enzymes and yeasts for biomass conversion; and DSM Advanced Solar, offering yield-boosting solutions for solar energy. The success or failure of these EBAs drives the strategic decisions on divestments and acquisitions to scale and change the business. (For more, listen to the interview with Rob van Leen,[11] chief innovation officer and executive board member of DSM.)

I believe figure 2 gives a diagonal view of process of aligning the proper purpose to the right process. Trying to do Horizon Three innovation with only current processes and capabilities (region A) is likely to be a risky investment of time and resources that are needed internally. You would also not expect to go into an external investment to learn about your current legacy business technology and pro-

---

11   Rob van Leen, DSM, Apr. 2012 and May 2017—Podcast Interviews.

cesses (region B). Along the spectrum, organizations are looking to determine an effective purpose and process, which will then drive the other aspects of the 5Ps.

PROCESS DESCRIPTIONS

There are a number of processes on the horizontal axis of figure 2. Following is a brief discussion of each of those that fall into Horizon Two and Horizon Three of purpose.

The position of process and purpose can vary by organization and by industry, and each should be explored in relation to the specific circumstance and strategy of a business considering corporate venturing.

- **Fund Investment.** A corporation can invest in a VC or private equity fund as a limited partner. Organizations often ask when—and why—this course of action is appropriate. Organizations can participate in one of these activities in the early stage of their venturing to understand the process and get to know the ecosystem and use it as an opportunity to see a wider deal flow. The relationship with the fund partners is important and will be discussed later. Other reasons for fund investments are due to the fund expertise in a specialist area (e.g., green technology, security tech). Fund investments with a geographic focus where the corporate has limited contacts is common in areas such as Israel and China, where regulation or not being part of the ecosystem makes it more difficult to directly invest. Investment in the likes of Tsing Capital and Emerald Technology are examples of this approach.

- **Corporate Venture Capital Fund.** A corporate can create a separate legal entity fund with a general partner (GP) to manage the fund while the corporate is the limited partner (LP). In this scenario, the corporation can help set the strategic parameters, but the fund is responsible for the investment and financial returns. The Tate & Lyle and REV Venture Partner funds are examples of this structure.

- **Direct Investment Corporate Venturing.** Corporate venturing is about identifying and scouting evolving technologies that expand or create new business models. A corporate can do the scouting directly for investment opportunities and subsequently invest directly off the balance sheet of the core parent organization. This process can be a quicker, more direct way of starting corporate venture capital (CVC) investing, but organizations should also understand the process and disciplines of investing. An understanding of the scale of the fund and the need to do follow-on investments is important for corporates to plan for. There are also reporting and accounting implications of the direct investment as they are reported within the parent organization. An organization that opts for corporate venturing processes often makes a minority stake investment of less than 20 percent to satisfy accounting consolidation rules so they do not have to report all the ups and downs of very small investments in their parent organization accounts. The majority of CVC organizations follow this direct off-balance-sheet approach to investing.

- **Incubation.** Incubation describes the act of an organization creating a unit—typically separate from its core business in both scope and location—that has the sole purpose of nurturing start-ups in creating new products or solutions in strategically adjacent industries. For incubation to be effective, it must be done relatively close to the current business of the parent corporation.

- **Mergers and Acquisitions.** Mergers and acquisitions are different from corporate venturing and partnering, as the business is acquired and usually brought into the processes and control of the parent organization. Many have described mergers and acquisitions as a "divorce," because the founders or controlling management team of the acquired business often leave after a short period of earn-out.

- **R&D.** R&D simply describes the scenario in which an organization approaches innovation by strategically funding its own R&D efforts to create new products or solutions to bring to market.

- **Spinouts.** If a corporation has a substantial amount of intellectual property such as patents or other interesting models that do not fit within its core business, those can be spun out into new organizations.

- **Corporate Partnering.** A corporation can partner with organizations in a number of ways—entering into a joint agreement, finding a new route to market, bringing a technology from one organization into the distribution channel for another, and so on. Corporate partnering can become more radical when Innovative New Value Chains are brought into the picture and an organization begins to partner to create entirely new business models.

- **University Partnering.** A corporation can partner with a university to fund R&D initiatives that might benefit its current or future business or to assist in training future developers or engineers for the current business. The position of university partnering can therefore vary across the spectrum, depending on the purpose, the university, and the people engaged.

Different processes used for different purposes can become multidimensional and are dependent on the market, available technology, and the industry. As I outlined earlier, different time lines exist by industry. The oil business, for example, could have two lines of business—upstream (focusing on raw material extraction) and downstream (the consumer side of the business). In this instance, the 5Ps vary widely between the upstream and downstream activities of a company. Upstream endeavors would involve dangerous and expensive activities such as extracting oil, and downstream endeavors would be retail focused—showing that some organizations can have different perspectives on where they fall within the spectrum of processes as they relate to purpose.

There is a coordinating role across the strategic innovation purpose and the processes under an executive board member. In some organizations, that executive board member could be the CEO if the company is going through a radical change or another executive member, such as the head of R&D or Strategy. Evonik[12] and DSM have

12 Bernhard Mohr and Peter Nagler, Evonik Ventures and CIO, Oct. 2013—Podcast Interview.

illustrated in my interviews a "chief innovation officer" executive coordinating role. Other organizations can coordinate similar activities with an innovation and venturing steering committee (or similarly termed group). Organizations must avoid having different processes reporting to different board members with different objectives—for example, fund investments reporting to Finance, Venture Fund reporting to Strategy, EBAs reporting to Marketing, and Open Innovation reporting to R&D. They are likely to be aligned to the functional objectives that could be more tactical to the current business operations and model, not addressing the strategic changes in the organization and industry. When a number of executives are brought together in a steering committee to guide the purpose, I have often heard them comment it was "the first time we have had a real 'strategic discussion.'" This is because the usual agenda is current operations or adjacent acquisitions of brands or country developments.

DIRECT CORPORATE VENTURING

Direct corporate venturing, briefly described earlier as the fund and direct investment CV, is key because it engages the organization directly in seeing tech, start-ups, and deal flow. It is also the most difficult model for today's executives to understand. Many organizations approach direct corporate venturing by making strategic minority stake investments in start-ups—offering insight that can allow stakeholders to better understand the trajectories of their respective markets.

Organizations will generally opt for direct corporate venturing when the business or technology in question is not mature enough to warrant a merger or acquisition. There are several rounds of investments in direct corporate venturing—seed investments, for example, are early-stage investments based largely on concept. Investments in the expansion stage follow market development and growth, often occurring in a series of follow-ons, or subsequent investments. In the investment rounds after seed investment, direct corporate venturing, an organization with a CVC unit may—and should—choose to invest alongside an established financial VC organization. This partnership provides the opportunity for the organization to gain assistance with due diligence, market testing, and the strategy behind applying benchmarks to the evaluation process. Figure 3 illustrates a "typical" model for a CVC fund.

Purpose	To gain an insight and be involved in new technology application and new business models that will disrupt an industry. In addition, provide a financial return for the venture activity.
Size of fund	Fund size of $100 million Call of $10-$15 million per year
Term of fund	Investment in 0-5 years, follow-on 3-5 years, 8-10 year life
Typical investments	Initial investment $1-$3 million, follow-on $3-$5 million Minority stake of 5%-15%, up to 20%
Number per year	Invest in 3-6 per year including follow-on Estimate 15-20 investments per fund
Lead or co-invest	Typically co-invest with financial VC and lead some Provide due diligence on technology and/or market
Team	Investment committee from corporate and "managing partners" Managing/general partners (manage 2-3 investments per year) Limited partner 100% corporate parent
Performance	Provide strategic insights on sectors, technology, and models Cash on cash, multiple return in 3-5 years on individual investments Fund return over the life of fund to be risk-weighted return after expenses

Figure 3

CORPORATE VENTURE CAPITAL—DIRECT INVESTMENT MODEL

It is important to understand that the process and structure of this model can vary considerably by industry, technology, geography, economic cycle, corporate aspirations, team capabilities, and more.

Organizations need to plan the size and structure of the fund to make it sustainable for investment. The purpose should identify the scope of interest, as with earlier examples such as Intel, Evonik, and BP. Different technologies, industries, and geographies will help to determine the size of the fund by understanding the typical round deal sizes. In this example, the $100 million fund will initially be investing up to $3 million per investment, in three to six investments. The ventures that are then growing would need additional funds and require follow-on investments. The investment managers will need to manage the investments after filtering hundreds of potential investments and could potentially sit on the boards of the businesses in which they have invested. The planning for the fund and resources to do the investments, and link the ventures to core business if appropriate, takes dedicated time and commitment over many years. This is a key role and was highlighted by Matt McElhattan[13] when, at Chevron Technology Ventures in May 2015, he felt the need to build capability and a team to connect to the core business implementation.

While the core techniques are similar—moving into a minority stake investment in a start-up and planning to follow on as it grows—investment types, time lines, and amounts vary widely by industry, geography, and technol-

13   Matt McElhattan, Chevron Technology Ventures, May 2015—Video Interview.

ogy. Investing in software and app creation, for example, requires less capital and a shorter investment duration than investing in medical development, which requires more time and often hinges on regulatory approval. Industrial processes are also likely to require more time and larger capital amounts to reach scale. Geography and industry also play roles. Investing in a technology start-up in Silicon Valley, for example, would be a different process than investing into a developing market in Eastern Europe or Shanghai. These markets have different maturity, and regulation has moved considerably in a short time.

What organizations setting up a CVC unit need to understand is that investing in start-ups is a risky and long-term commitment. This is not dissimilar from launching new products, many of which also do not succeed. In the case of early-stage investments, many VCs say that six out of ten are likely to fail, two will return investors' money, and two will provide a significant return. These are of course averages and the better funds tend to have more winners, as success breeds success with better managers attracting better deals and investment partners. The challenge for corporates is to understand that the failures are likely to occur earlier and investors need to build up a portfolio and build on success. You will consistently lose money if you enter and leave corporate venture investing on short cycles.

An organization can start on the journey with a structure, while understanding how it will likely evolve. Organizations have started with small funds and grown. Others have started with fully funded GP/LP funds, and still others have started with poor structure and poor commitment that failed within a few years, before returning a number of months later to try again.

To truly gain strategic insights, organizations need to understand that the benefit comes from the determining theme and Innovative New Value Chain hypothesis, by scanning the market, and developing propositions. Making the investments shows commitment to the ecosystem and provides the detailed understanding of the ventures and the dynamic in the start-up and the market. Even if the specific investment does not make a return—which will more than likely be the case—there is still significant value in these insights. The knowledge gained and shared will help to support the strategic direction of the organization, decisions on emerging business areas, and input to acquisition and disposal decisions. Tony Askew,[14] founding managing partner of REV Venture Partners, talks powerfully about this, as Reed Elsevier (now called RELX) transformed into an online data business and is continuing the transformation.

---

14   Tony Askew, REV Venture Partners, Jul. 2016—Podcast Interview.

The fund also needs to be considered in the wider context of the 5Ps for an organization (see figure 4).

Making Deal Flow Strategic

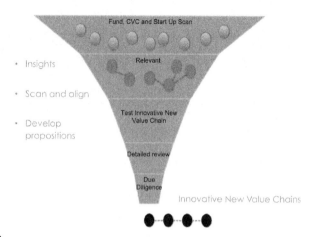

Figure 4

TATE & LYLE: A CASE FOR DIRECT INVESTMENT

Tate & Lyle is a food and beverage company that was historically focused on bulk sugar processing. When Chief Executive Iain Ferguson set up the Tate & Lyle Venture Fund, the team began to look at how the market was moving toward an industry with lower-volume, higher-value ingredients. Tate & Lyle identified two new individuals to run the fund and invested a relatively small amount into its first venturing endeavor—£50 million over a ten-year period. The fund has been a success, and the industry insights Tate & Lyle can glean from this activity in other markets, as explained in an interview with David Atkinson,[15] are most valuable.

David Atkinson, managing partner, Tate & Lyle Ventures LP, gave me an update from when I originally worked with Tate & Lyle and the CVC unit in the early 2000s. A case study about Tate & Lyle also appeared in my 2006 book, *Open Innovation in Action: How to Be Strategic in the Search for New Sources of Value.*

"Back in 2006, few corporates in the food sector were operating venture funds. Those that did were in-house and managed off-the-balance sheet, apart from Nestlé-backed Inventages that had a much wider brief than its corporate backer. It is to the credit and vision of Tate & Lyle's then-CEO, Iain Ferguson, who had already been instrumental in setting up Unilever's venturing activities, that Tate & Lyle Ventures [TLV] was born. Operating as an independent fund and externally managed by Circadia Ventures LLP, the structure of the fund has changed little to this day, despite the inevitable changes of personnel at the corporate including a new CEO, Javed Ahmed, in 2009. Fast forward to 2017, and a number of FMCG [fast-moving consumer goods] groups have now estab-

15   David Atkinson, Tate & Lyle Ventures, Mar. 2013—Podcast Interview.

lished their own venture fund units, especially in the United States, with a variety of operating models: in-house, externally managed, or a hybrid.

What lessons have we learned over the last decade for managing a successful corporate venture fund? We have identified a few key aspects, which have remained a constant during those years and across both of the funds Circadia operates for Tate & Lyle.

1. **A simple structure.** TLV is structured just like any other independent venture capital fund. This is a structure that all potential investee companies and, crucially, other investors recognize and feel comfortable with.

2. **The relationship with the corporate is transparent.** For example, Tate & Lyle holds no special rights or requirements regarding, say, internal sponsorship with a potential investee company before agreeing to investment.

3. **A simple decision-making process.** Potential investee companies see corporates as slow decision-making bodies; this puts them at a disadvantage in venture capital. TLV's Investment Committee meets monthly to make quick invest-

ment decisions; more regular meetings can be called as necessary.

4. **A clear pre-agreed scope.** The corporate and the manager should fully debate and discuss the remit of the fund before launch. This needs to be a balance between corporate strategy and the fund's requirement for sustainable and investable deal flow. It is important to get senior-level engagement because, with a fund life of up to ten years, corporate strategy can change quicker than that of the fund's scope!

5. **Engagement with all levels of the corporate structure.** As important as it is to have high-level executive buy-in and support, wider engagement and understanding of the fund's aims throughout the organization is vital.

6. **Clear and quick response.** Not every opportunity will fit with the fund's ambitions or scope, especially when the fund is as focused as TLV on food sciences and technologies. That said, clear, quick, and helpful feedback to prospective partners is important, especially when you are often the most visible part of the innovation program of the corporate.

Ultimately, TLV's success can be put down to a balancing of Tate & Lyle's strategic aims and ambitions with regards to innovation in the food sector, with the discipline and focus on financial return of the venture capital fund. It has served us well for over a decade so far."

INDIRECT CORPORATE VENTURING FUNDS

Indirect corporate venturing describes a process by which an organization invests in a separate financial venture capital (VC) fund—one still aligned with its purpose, of course—instead of a direct investment in the start-up itself. This approach brings the potential for industry insight and expertise in technology and geography. In addition, some funds allow investing organizations to have associates participate in conducting due diligence or stimulating deal flow, bringing stakeholders close to the investment ecosystems and scouting cycles of unfamiliar yet relevant industry sectors.

To understand how an indirect corporate venturing fund operates, one must first understand that a typical VC fund is structured such that it raises money that it will then invest in start-ups. Generally, managing partners take approximately 2 percent per annum of the investment amount for administration fees. At the end of the life of the term, the profit is distributed to the limited partners. In some situations, the partners could have a 20 percent carry—that is, an agreement in which 80 percent of the surplus from the fund after expenses goes back to the limited partner investors as profit while the remaining 20 percent goes to the managing partners, who also might have invested a small amount into the fund personally.

An indirect investment allows an organization to be a limited partner in the above scenario, seeing a potential return while strategically gaining access into new geographic markets. For example, investing organizations can access expertise on local culture, regulation, language, currency, and more. Investing in Israeli funds, industrial technology in Emerald Technology Fund, or China's Tsinghua Capital Fund are key examples of ways in which organizations can diversify and build partnerships in emerging markets.

Paul Morris,[16] who set up the Dow Venture fund and more recently worked with the UK government's Department for International Trade, has outlined in more detail the approaches to formal or informal relationships between corporates and VC investors.

---

16   Paul Morris, UKTI, May 2015—Video Interview.

DUE DILIGENCE AND VALUATIONS

An important part of the process for corporates in doing minority early-stage investments is doing the due diligence and valuation of an early-stage, often pre-revenue business that is making losses. The metrics that are often used in mergers and acquisitions of profitable businesses with net present value, discounted cash flows, and multiples of earnings are not valid. In the case of early-stage investment, the valuation is related to the size of investment that is required to develop the business to the next stage in order to acquire a minority stake in the business. The investor then has to judge whether that investment would give an expected multiple return. At a valuations workshop I ran, a number of speakers suggested a "rule of thumb" to determine the amount of money needed to develop the business over twelve to eighteen months for under 20 percent of the equity/stock: the expected multiple of return should be times three the investment. Helping the corporate venturing team, the investment committee, and the wider organization understand the difference in approaches is important. There are approaches that organizations can take to put off the valuation until a later round of investment, as it is critical to understand that an over- or undervaluation can have implications for future rounds and motivation of the team.

The valuation and due diligence also has to take into

account the fact that the outcome will be the start-up and the investor embarking on a long-term relationship, and so the impact of a poor deal can have implications. In the case of a mergers and acquisitions negotiation, the founders are likely to be leaving and the ongoing relationship is not likely to be as important.

Due diligence, valuation, and case study could be the focus of a full program, so I do not want to go into too much detail or give too many examples in this book.

MERGERS AND ACQUISITIONS

Done strategically and in a manner that aligns with an organization's innovation purpose, completing a merger or acquisition can be a valuable business decision. Some corporates directly invest in start-ups with the hope of eventually acquiring or merging with that business entirely. While these instances do occur, they are rare and vary among sectors. A business in the pharmaceutical industry, for example, might move from concept to clinical trials before being acquired by a large corporation that was not necessarily an investor. An area to be considered in the realm of mergers and acquisitions is that start-ups can be oversupported or have inappropriate processes imposed by large corporates once absorbed, eventually smothering them.

Pursuing CVC, as I have outlined, provides great insights and opportunities to understand the rapidly changing technology and business models in a sector. This is important knowledge to be used in the strategic direction of the business to inform acquisition and disposal decisions. Insights into a sector will also be important for the integration of acquisitions.

Direct investment can also be an effective approach, allowing organizations to make minority stake investments in strings of start-ups that become Innovative New Value Chains. Those organizations can then create private equity deals to consolidate those businesses, using an acquisition strategy to bring together multiple start-ups. We will see good cases of this in the later section on Innovative New Value Chains.

INCUBATION

Investing (either directly or indirectly) in or acquiring a start-up are not the only processes organizations can use to foster growth and innovation. Incubation is an alternative that organizations can use to gather insight around the start-ups and technologies poised to disrupt their industries.

Plug and Play describes itself as a global innovation platform for start-ups, corporations, and investors. Every year, it reviews 5,000 start-ups, invests in over 160, and runs industry-specific accelerator programs. There are 150 corporate partners to the start-ups that are directly impacting their space. These introductions help both parties thrive together through investments, pilots, and acquisitions.

In this scenario, the corporates are not necessarily making direct investments but are partnering or supporting. Some organizations hold their own incubator competitions to gather new technologies in certain sectors or certain locations. Winners come into the incubator and get paid to work on ideas applicable to the area.

Many corporates tend to move in and out of incubation strategies too quickly, not seeing the benefits. It is true that sometimes incubation is not a clear fit into the current business model for an organization.

One example of an organization that has a broad overview in the incubation space is Unilever Foundry. Its process is to work globally with different incubators and partners to identify and support start-ups that will support the future areas for their business. In one example, they put €100,000 into a South African start-up to bring tech to Europe through SMS—that is, text—via mobile advertising. The exposure and investment helps validate the technology for the start-up, and the investors are satisfied because it is new revenue generation that does not dilute their equity in the deal. Ultimately, the start-up provides insights into new technologies and brings a new approach to the marketplace. As the propositions are close to the current core business of the parent organization, they can involve marketing or R&D from corporate. You can learn about the process in an interview with Unilever Foundry.[17]

KEY MESSAGES

Processes need to be effective to deliver the purpose. I've described a range of processes, some of which are further away from the core business and more open to more technology, start-ups, and partners that can give insights and opportunities for corporates. CVC is one process that gives corporates direct engagement with some of the most innovative and disruptive areas.

There are many start-ups being set up to apply new technology—new business models to address a market insight they have seen. Many will not succeed, and those that do will create significant value. Seeing the deal flow, identifying start-ups to invest in, and being involved in such growth through incubation, partnering, and more provides great insights. Even if the business itself does not

---

17 Jeremy Basset, Unilever Foundry, Jun. 2015—Podcast Interview.

succeed, the process provides knowledge on technology, markets, and models that will influence the core business and bring success for other investments in the portfolio.

4. PEOPLE: THE CENTRAL RESOURCE

Do feel free to share!
@agaule

Corporates typically put process at the center of inno-vation and organization, but start-ups recognize that *people* actually challenge and change processes—that's why people are central to innovation around which the 5Ps flow. Those running a corporate venturing and open-innovation process help determine the strategic purpose and ongoing alignment for those activities. An organiza-tion might start with a Horizon Two purpose, for example, but must have the right leaders with gravitas who are willing to look ahead to the future of their industry.

People are important at every level of innovation and corporate venturing, not just at the executive level. To make minority stake investments, for example, corporates must find people with the external perspective and keen ability to work with partners such as VCs, aligning their performance, their initiatives, and their remuneration to the success of the start-ups and partners.

This skill set can be summed up in a term I coined in my first book, *Open Innovation in Action*:[18] successful corporate venturing requires the work of *extrapreneurs*. Extrapreneurs in a corporate have both extra entrepreneurial and venture capital (VC) skills, and they have *external* perspective to understand how corporate actions align with strategic objectives. They are key players in determining the "exit" strategy for innovations—whether that exit takes the form of a spinout company, a joint venture, or an in-house launch among an organization's existing products and services. They have a vision of where a venture should be headed in the medium- to long term.

---

18 Andrew Gaule, *Open Innovation in Action: How to Be Strategic in the Search for New Sources of Value* (H-I Network, 2006). http://amazon.co.uk/ Open-Innovation-Action-Strategic-Sources/dp/0955111714.

PEOPLE AS A HIVE

You can compare people in strategic innovation and venturing to bees in a hive, as I outlined in my previous book and in the *Financial Times*:

> *We have seen that organizations need to think of their chief executives as queen bees sitting in a complex organizational hive. Leading organizations need to have "scout" workers and partners who can identify new market and technology opportunities. Learning a corporate "waggle dance" to develop strategy is far better than traditional consultants who spend their time looking at current markets.*[19]

Having a good sense for the environment and being able to communicate effectively at a senior level to influence the organization are key skills for innovation and CV leaders. I see this organic metaphor as showing that relationships are important.

THE ROLE OF INNOVATION IN LEADERSHIP

Some large corporates have benefited from charismatic leaders with a strong eye for innovation—take Elon Musk

---

19 Andrew Gaule, "Join Hands in Corporate Waggle Dance," *Financial Times*, November 2, 2009, http://www.ft.com/cms/s/0/346930ae-c74f-11de-bb6f-00144feab49a.html?ft_site=falcon&desktop=true.

of Tesla, Jeff Bezos of Amazon, Jack Ma of Alibaba, and Arianna Huffington of the *Huffington Post*, for instance. Other organizations have been faced with challenges in their specific industries, requiring their leaders to adapt by innovating for survival. One leader who excelled in this respect is Crispin Davis, chief executive of Reed Elsevier Group from 1999 to 2009.

In his early days of leadership, Davis recognized that his business, which had historically published professional industry-focused paper journals, would not survive in the age of online media. Within twelve years, Reed Elsevier Group (now called RELX) had shifted 80 percent of its revenue from paper-journal to online-journal production. Currently, the business's corporate venturing unit is exploring decision-support applications involving emerging technologies such as big data and artificial intelligence.

Executives like Davis have grasped a key concept of success in innovation: corporate venture capital (CVC) managers and executives must communicate at the appropriate level and time, and those who implement the venturing strategy must consider that insight. DSM is another example of an organization mastering this balance, as its structure allows for the strategic sharing of insights from those overseeing direct fund investments to R&D.

THE DYNAMIC BETWEEN A CORPORATION AND A VENTURE TEAM

There are more ways than one for teams to function, of course. Some corporates have sub-boards of executive committees or forums where business units come together to agree on Horizon Three strategies. The key is communication. Innovation pursued in silos is far less worthwhile than innovation pursued as part of a larger strategy.

Perhaps nowhere is this need for communication more evident than in the dynamic between a corporate parent and the venture team when a direct corporate venturing model is being used. The venture team must have a balance of skills, including basic VC skills such as the ability to flesh out and pursue deals. They may be examining potential technologies and capabilities of a thousand or more start-ups, doing due diligence on one hundred, investing in a few, and sitting on the boards of some of these. Those numbers are examples, but they show the required capacity and breadth of responsibility of venture team leaders.

It is also critical for the venture team to understand and be able to bring in capabilities from the corporate parent, carefully selecting technologies to pursue that are either very close to or radically different from the current business model, depending on strategy. Often, venture teams comprise a balance of internal and external team members. Organizations pursuing Horizon Three innovations generally have a larger external representation because they are looking for capabilities outside of their core business models, whereas organizations falling in Horizon Two have higher internal representation. Industries with a higher asset base, such as oil and industrial business, have longer development times that tend to require more internal resource and alignment.

Generally, venturing teams should be lean, keeping overhead light. Otherwise, when reorganizations occur, corporate venture groups could be cut. Dominique Mégret[20] of Swisscom ventures made this point clearly by recommending, "keep the team as small as possible... to show you can cover your costs."

VENTURE TEAM

Venture teams examine technologies and business models with the goal of bringing insight back to the corporate parent, ultimately inspiring action while also making financial returns. For this to occur, proper role management within venture teams is critical. This is an overview of three of the key roles (see also figure 5):

---

20 Dominique Mégret, Swisscom, Jul. 2016—Video Interview.

Corporate and Venture Team

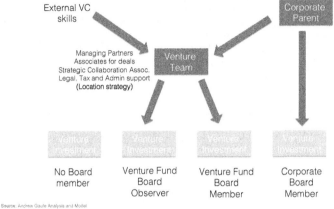

Source: Andrew Gaule Analysis and Model

Figure 5

· **Managing partners** are individuals who manage the
operation of the venturing unit. Similar to managing
partners in VC funds, they should be in their roles for
at least seven years to see through the investment,
growth, and exit for optimal returns. There are generally two to three managing partners of a venture
team, depending on size and scope.

· **Investment directors** are often board members or
observers within an investee company. Depending on
the size of the group, there can be five or six directors,
all of whom should remain in their roles for more than
five years to see returns.

- **Investment associates,** or theme leaders, often rotate into venture teams from other departments such as R&D or mergers and acquisitions. They often plan to be in this role for approximately two years before cycling back into the corporate parent.

The noted longevity of various venture team members in their roles is a critical detail in this discussion. To build relationships, understand the market, make deals, and do the requisite follow-on investments, organizations must play close attention to how long key people are in their roles. Organizations that start corporate venturing and proceed to move managing partners or directors to different roles too quickly will not succeed because they have not maintained the continuity necessary to achieve a thorough understanding of changes in the marketplace or been in the role sufficiently long enough to see an investment through to maturity and exit.

Organizations like Swisscom, led by Dominique Mégret, understand that corporate venturing units evolve over time as trust and capabilities build. In a video interview with me, Mégret very powerfully spoke of seeing CVC leadership as a career choice, with growth in the role as the strategy and the portfolio develop. He also believes the CVC unit needs to be considered a business and should maintain a small cost-focused team to be able to deliver financial and strategic returns. This can then provide the credibility and trust within the organization to be able to develop the portfolio over a three-to-five-year period. During this time, the CVC leader also has to educate around the investment, steering committees and businesses on the dynamics and pace of the investment when the corporation is not in the lead.

William (Bill) Taranto, too, brought his experience from a similar fund in Johnson & Johnson to his role at Merck. He knew the ecosystem and the technologies at play, and he brought his credibility and relationships with him as he transitioned roles to build the requisite trust. We will hear more about Taranto later as we look at driving Innovative New Value Chains in chapter seven.

SITTING ON THE BOARD OF A START-UP

After the venture team has done due diligence on many start-ups and opted to invest in one, it is not uncommon for individuals from the team to sit on the board of the start-up. Members of the corporate venture team will have fiduciary duties on the board, helping the start-up build its capabilities and generate revenue; it is their duty to ensure the success of the start-up. This can involve bringing the skills, experience, contacts, and connections to the corporate parent in order to help in that role. The board members gain strategic insight into shifting technologies and business models through the eyes of the start-up. It must, however, be stressed that company-specific confidential information must remain confidential to the board and the start-up.

While sitting on the board of a start-up, venture team members communicate with stakeholders, including founders, additional corporate investors, and a number of other interested parties. For this reason, selected team members must be people-oriented and possess the attitudes and attributes required to help an early-stage start-up navigate the sometimes-chaotic world of technology testing and rapid change. Jan Harley,[21] investment director for Unilever Ventures, has spoken about these issues while sitting on the board for BrainJuicer (now called System1 Group). I, along with John Kearon, the founder and CEO of BrainJuicer, am pleased that these insights are featured as a case study from which new corporate venture members are learning.

It is possible for members of the corporate parent to sit on the board of a start-up—*possible*, yet not always recommended. An examination of the legalities of this scenario is provided in chapter nine; the key issue for this discussion is the potential contamination of intellectual property.

---

21   Jan Harley, Unilever Ventures, Jan. 2017—Video Interview.

There is also the need to ensure the board member has the skills, contacts, and attributes relevant for a start-up, as opposed to the skills of an operational manager. When a VC team member sits on a board, they have fiduciary duties to the *venture*, not the corporate parent. If a member of the corporate parent sits on that same board, they must take care to make that distinction as well. Failing to meet these criteria can lead to inappropriate behaviors and potential liabilities. If there is going to be a collaboration or commercial relationship between the corporate and the venture unit, I would recommend this be dealt with via a separate agreement related to the R&D, marketing, supply chain, or other area of work.

Essentially, if a member of the investing corporation wishes to sit on the board of a start-up in which it has invested through its corporate venturing arm, they must have the skills to support a small start-up, be cognizant of the intellectual property risks, and know whether to have the corporation or the start-up in mind when contributing to decisions.

BOARDS BEHAVING BADLY

Proper board behavior is critical to both the success of the start-up and of the investment(s). Conversely, improper board behavior can lead to struggles. I am familiar with one instance of a board behaving badly. In this example, I knew the CVC, the VC, and the start-up very well.

The parties had already gone through the initial seed investments, so a round of financing had been completed. The start-up had proven the technology, and it was time to expand into industry testing. In this instance, testing was to be lengthy and could take many years to fully scale up, so the start-up needed investors to follow on with subsequent investments.

Before additional funding was secured, though, the role of managing partner of the corporate venture fund, previously filled by a European, was now filled by a corporate individual in the United States who was more familiar with large private equity deals than early-stage seed investment. More than that changed, though—the strategic scope of the corporation shifted after the personnel switch. As a result, the board participation of this particular CVC partner declined. The partner began asking for increasing amounts of information from the start-up and the board before eventually deciding not to follow on. Not only that, they were also uncooperative in signing documents that would allow other investors to follow on in their absence.

Now, the start-up was running out of money, and the CVC was effectively vetoing the fund-raising. The other investors were willing to invest, but the corporation was not. Then, the VC investor wrote a letter to the chairman of the board of the CVC corporate's holding company indicating it had stifled the start-up. Eventually, the CVC team opted to exit the deal to the other shareholders at a discounted valuation. Today, the head of the corporate venture unit and the CEO of the operating company are no longer in their jobs. This is not necessarily due to the investment, but it illustrates the fact that the CEO and CVC leader roles are often on a shorter life cycle than the time to exit an investment. The start-up is profitable and continues to develop with more time to go before an exit.

There are two lessons one can take away from the story of the board that behaved badly, and they both circle back to longevity: First, understanding that investments are meant to be long term, and that follow-ons will be required, is critical in making a return. Second, communicating the premise and long-term potential gains of corporate venturing is imperative, especially when corporate leadership inevitably changes.

There are many other cases where board activity does not go *badly* wrong but, rather, where executives from corporates are not effective. For example, executives may have inappropriate skills or the wrong attitude to work with start-ups. They may also become too involved in day-to-day operations, fail to differentiate their investor role from their board role, or leak intellectual property.

REMUNERATION

An important discussion under the topic of people in the 5Ps is remuneration and rewards. Often, individuals within a corporate venture unit have remuneration packages aligned to the corporate parent, including traditional provisions such as equity-based bonuses. In other instances, remuneration packages are aligned to the fees and carried interest on the funds. Typically, venture fund fees are 2 percent per annum of fund value, to cover all salaries and administrative costs. Carried interest is typically up to 20 percent of the profits of the fund and becomes payable once the investors have been repaid their original investment plus a defined hurdle rate. (A full glossary of terms is available.[22]) When the investments make profitable returns, then, so do those individuals in the corporate venture unit. These types of rewards do not materialize until the end of the fund, if ever.

J. Thelander Consulting completes an annual survey of senior executives and those in corporate venturing to better understand their standard remuneration packages. The 2016 Corporate Venture Capital Compensation

---

22 Find a glossary containing these and other terms at Aimava.com/resources.

Survey (featured in the World of Corporate Venturing 2017 annual review from Mawsonia) compiled data from 175 corporate venturing executives representing 125 leading programs. On average, CVC unit leaders earned $337,500 annually, including a $150,000 cash bonus.

Besides providing baseline data on compensation in the industry, the Thelander report also pointed to a trend: The bonus pool is increasingly becoming more aligned to the financial returns of the CVC fund. Only 11 percent of respondents, in fact, indicated they had a fee and carry package. Also interesting is that 60 percent of the senior executives surveyed had come to their current CVC unit from an external VC firm, rather than being recruited from within the corporate parent.

There are many approaches corporate venturing units and corporate parents can take when it comes to people, and there are pros and cons to all of them. The key is finding a setup—from the executive makeup of the unit to how they are remunerated—that strategically aligns with the identified purpose and process.

KEY MESSAGES

People are central to determining the strategic direction and alignment, leading processes over a long term and interacting with partners to drive the financial and strategic purpose of an organization. Balancing the people-related considerations within a strategic innovation and corporate venturing is critical. When you are driving innovation and supporting a start-up, you need to show you are in the same boat, navigating the rapids of technology, business, and market building to hopefully lead to success.

5. PARTNERS: CREATING STRONG RELATIONSHIPS

Do feel free to share!
@agaule

When an organization has clarity of purpose and process, it can determine the partners and be clearer on the respective roles. In the process chapter, I discussed how the different approaches to innovation activities typically work with partners and collaborators. These include venture capitalists, corporate venturing units, universities, or incubators, for example.

Organizations that wish to innovate are by definition participating in activities outside their capabilities. Therefore, they need partners in order to deliver solutions and grow capabilities internally. These two go hand in hand.

The language used when discussing partnering is important to the success of the endeavor. For organizations that have formed poor partnerships in the past, the very word *partnering* can cause hesitancy. It is important to differentiate that partnering is *not* the same as simply outsourcing or creating a full joint venture from the current business.

I often see outsourcing as a core business approach. If an organization's executives have found a partner to whom they are comfortable outsourcing the catering for an event, for example, those executives know how many meals to order, and they know generally how the arrangement will turn out. Partnering in a corporate venturing sense on the path to creating Innovative New Value Chains is more of a journey—one in which the destination is not clearly defined and in which all partners share both risks and rewards. In this instance, the relationship is more of a strategic alliance built on the right combination of people and trust. Some in the industry refer to this level of partnership as a marriage.

PARTNERSHIPS AND PROCESSES

Different partnerships are appropriate for different processes. When organizations work with funds to invest in start-ups, for example, they are partnered via venture capital and private equity. There is more to it than that, though—when either executives from corporate parents or, more commonly, VC team members sit on boards for those start-ups, they are invested in the success of that business. They are working to raise funding and offering input and advice. Remember, those board appointments may take many years—a long time to build a relationship. It does not stop there. Eventually, start-ups can partner with other start-ups to create value chains. Again, building relationships and capabilities outside the core business is key because it is not always clear how, or if, these value chains will perform. A core-business-style transactional approach of a service purchase or acquisition will not create the necessary alignment or shared rewards.

Mergers and acquisitions processes often do not have the "marriage-like" partnerships that direct or indirect corporate venturing do. Generally, in fact, mergers and acquisitions are often called "divorce agreements" because founders and leaders leave in exchange for payment.

There are other types of innovation-based relationships that are categorized as partnerships, such as incubators.

When a corporate parent opts to run an incubator outside of its physical environment, for example, there is an obvious need for trust and partnership.

ROLES OF PARTNERS

The types and degree of partnering will vary depending on investment phases. Partnering with and investing in a start-up still in the seed phase, for example, requires nurturing and support. This situation is entirely different from investing in a company that could potentially be moving toward a late-stage private equity acquisition. Neither is incorrect, nor is any strategy in the middle—the importance, remember, is alignment.

FORMAL AND INFORMAL INVESTMENTS WITH PARTNERS

A formal corporate venturing investment relationship refers to a corporation acting as a limited partner investor in a venture capital fund. Corporates can also invest informally when they invest alongside a VC unit or another financial investor for a specific deal.

There are a number of reasons why a corporate would invest as a limited partner (LP) in a fund and a number of benefits to doing so.

It can be the first stage in getting involved in corporate venturing and provides experience in being involved in the ecosystem. The corporate will need to review the sectors the fund invests in and the fund's openness to sharing insights on the deal flow and investments they make. This can vary by fund, ranging from minimal visibility on the investments made, to access and working on due diligence for the investments. Funds that want to work more closely with corporates may allow corporates to place investment associates in the fund office.

Investing in a fund can enhance deal flow insights and potential opportunities to invest alongside the fund in an investment syndicate. The fund also provides sector expertise such as special materials, clean tech, or artificial intelligence. An expertise in a geography is often another important case for investing a fund. This has been an important reason for investing in funds in Israel and China, where the ecosystems can be specialist or difficult to enter as an external investor.

A fund may also be a complementary group of corporates and financial investors that have a joint interest in a sector. An example is Aster Capital, which has investment from Alstom, Solvay, Schneider Electric, and the European Investment Fund. This approach allows the sharing of management costs as well as allowing opportunities for collaboration in common areas of interest that are not competitive.

Investment in a fund provides the benefits of the expertise and management in a budget but does not give the direct insights that come from the deal flow and due diligence.

Investing informally has its benefits: having an investing partner, for example, helps the corporate to understand the deal by allowing the venture capital organization to perform due diligence and validate the deal terms, both of which help lessen the appearance of "dumb money." In addition, informal partnerships can pool and syndicate risks, help provide new capabilities for start-ups to succeed, and generate other exit options.

The notion of additional exit options is an important one. The investing corporation can sometimes be seen as the kiss of death for a start-up for two reasons: there can be concerns about leakage of intellectual capital, and the investment can be seen as limiting the start-up's only path forward. In the case of boards behaving badly, for example, the success of the start-up was contingent on follow-on investments from investors, which became complicated by changes in corporate strategy and personnel.

Paul Morris of the Department of International Trade in

the United Kingdom, in corporate venturing academies I have led, has spoken about formal and informal partnerships; a video synopsis can be found in the resources.[23] CVC cannot and should not avoid being involved with VC organizations, as they bring benefits to the start-up ecosystem. Morris has also described the "prenuptial agreement": an open, honest exchange prior to committing to invest in the fund. Is the fund general partner able and willing to deliver what the corporate fund needs over the long term? You should also meet the "family and friends"—the partners, other limited partners, and some of their investee companies. This could be a six- to twelve-month assessment, involving one-on-one meetings and fund investor meetings. Once you have invested in a fund or have built an informal relationship, you need to nurture and grow the ongoing relationship. If members of the CVC team change, this task can become especially challenging.

As an example of the interconnected nature of partnering, Evonik Venture Capital has six fund investments,[24] including specialist funds in energy (e.g., Emerald Technology Ventures), regional local funds (e.g., Gründerfonds Ruhr), and Chinese funds (e.g., Hosen Capital). Along with Evonik, the Emerald fund has other corporates investing

---

23 Paul Morris UKTI May 2015 video interview

24 "Portfolio Companies," *Evonik*, http://venturing.evonik.com/sites/venturing/en/portfolio-companies/Pages/fund-investments.aspx.

as limited partners, including ABB, Henkel, Michelin, and SABIC.

Chapter ten shows in detail the interconnected nature of doing direct investments alongside VCs in a syndicate. As an example, in 2016 Intel invested with Alphabet Ventures, GE, Qualcomm, Kleiner Perkins Caufield & Byers, and Sequoia Capital on many occasions.

KEY MESSAGES: KEY TO PARTNERING

Building relationships and partnerships to do joint investments and then helping to nurture and exit an investment is key. You need to get the best deal flow and secure good terms to make financially rewarding strategic deals. The relationship between a financial VC and CVC has been compared to a couple ballroom dancing. The financial VC is leading; it has clarity of objective that is financially focused. The CVC often has other strategic objectives and processes that are determined by the corporate. It can often be thought of as dancing backward in high heels.

Partnering is effective for investments, but it is also a critical component of building Innovative New Value Chains. Corporates must understand that the potentials of partnering go beyond single start-ups; orchestrating strategic alignment across a string of start-ups rooted in different geographies or focused on new technologies, for example, can allow more significant growth than would be possible from partnering with a VC organization alone.

6. PERFORMANCE: MEASURING SUCCESS

Do feel free to share!
@agaule

We want our purpose to drive our process and the other parameters in the 5Ps, and then we want to measure the performance. In the earlier chapters, we outlined some of the benefits we were looking for. Now, we wish to measure whether we are achieving those outcomes.

Organizations are likely to look to survive as technology and new business models disrupt their industries and business lines. For example, electric vehicles, distributed energy, online retailing, digital photography, and IP telephony are causing or have caused radical change in industries. So if you innovate and venture into new business areas you can survive. Building new sustainable business lines, products, and services is also a key purpose that you wish to measure. The challenge comes from the fact that insights, specific knowledge, and deals will feed into the decisions that result in strategic change. Within an organization, these changes require many inputs from stakeholders to devise a plan for effective implementation. As you can imagine, claiming the credit for the input of the corporate venturing effort can be a challenge when it is a team effort.

On the next level of core business benefit insights, investments and collaborations can provide the direct benefits of increased sales, lower cost, and more effective use of assets. There is still the challenge of attributing the input from specific engagements and venturing, as, again, a team effort is required to be successful. I will address this challenge further in the chapter.

The financial returns from an investment and the value of a portfolio of investments can be measured but usually after a long period, as technology and investment take many years to make a return. Materiality is then a challenge for many corporates, as the direct financial return may give a multiple return—for example, a $100 million fund over ten years—that is still small relative to the many billions of dollars in revenue and profit that might occur quarterly in a global corporate.

It is the balancing of these strategic and financial performance measurements of success of innovation and corporate venturing initiatives that we will be considering. Usually, the primary performance consideration is what kind of strategic insight and benefit is gained through the venturing process. This is, however, not easily determined. A corporation, for example, can examine a portfolio of investments—one with thousands of interactions, hundreds of instances of due diligence, and five to ten investments—and have a high-level, strategic discussion as a result. This information allows corporates to examine data at a portfolio level, identifying industry themes they can then use to generate strategic decision making and develop significant opportunities. In an earlier chapter, we saw the funnel image of deal opportunities under review, due diligence, and investment all giving insights. This is important when we are considering the industry and organizational changes discussed in Horizon Three. Delivering strategic future change needs to be differentiated from delivering the short- and medium-term objectives of business units, which I would describe as tactical. It is important to consider how we keep the broader scouting capabilities and deliver results instead of getting dragged into details on individual and ad hoc investments.

Performance is also measured in terms of financial returns. The metrics here are relatively straightforward—most of the time, that is. Financial returns for a fund are usually calculated as a return on capital after a cost of capital rate and after expenses. In the VC community, the performance of the fund managers is then ranked against comparable funds, in geographies and similar time periods. The challenge for CVCs trying this approach is that the fund is likely to be early in its life cycle, investing in new areas and sectors that may not have comparable data. For example, an organization I worked with in the early 2000s, doing consumer-sector investments (well ahead of other venture capital organizations), would have no comparison on which to base the performance of its financial returns.

Compare that example to the likes of Intel Capital, one of the world's longest-running funds. At a program I ran in January 2017, the company stated that it had invested $11.8 billion in nearly 1,500 companies in 57 countries since 1991. With this scale and capacity, Intel Capital is able to track the financial returns by investment, investment managers, time, and geography.

In an interview with Abdul Guefor,[25] an investment director at Intel Capital, I asked the following: How do you measure the benefit of Intel Capital to the business in hard and softer metrics?

Guefor replied, "In my treasury role, we measure internal rate of return [IRR—a measure of annual financial performance] and cash-on-cash returns, as all investors do. The strategic benefits that accrue to Intel are as important, and these are more difficult to quantify. We have worked on having a range of measures that had a strategic milestone focus, but these became too bureaucratic and did not add that much value. We run a profit-and-loss approach of accounting—as Intel does off-balance-sheet investment—and we also run a shadow accounting structure to enable us to do a comparison of a fund investment with costs and carry to enable us to indicate an IRR and cash-on-cash return metric, comparable to the VC stats. Ultimately, we have found that asking our business partners is the best way to measure the strategic benefits. We regularly talk to the heads of the business units at Intel that we work with, and they grade us on whether we have helped them, both in devising their strategies as well as with investments and how we can do better."

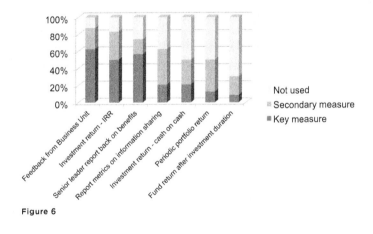

Figure 6

25 Abdul Guefor, Intel Capital, Feb. 2012—Podcast Interview.

I conducted a survey of leading corporate venture units to determine the types of measures they use (see figure 6). It was interesting to see there is not a one-size-fits-all approach to measuring the performance of corporate venturing efforts. Rather, using a combination of big-picture strategic and granular financial metrics is often the best path forward.

Many experienced leaders of CVC units will echo the following sentiment: "You do not stay strategic for long unless you make a financial return!" I would also say that a CVC unit needs to show it can make an investment and get a bigger cash amount back than it invested. This should also aim to be achieved on a time scale that meets the needs of that parent organization. Corporates may have a time perspective of a few years, not understanding that the investment cycle of a fund requires the patience to wait more than ten years for a fund to complete its cycle. They also may not understand that it takes a number of years to become an evergreen fund—that is, an investment fund that does not have a specified end date whereby returns are made available for reinvestment.[26]

---

26 Find a glossary containing these and other terms at Aimava.com/resources.

THE PORTFOLIO AND PERFORMANCE APPROACHES

Organizations often start off on a journey of innovation and venturing without monitoring the portfolio and engagement in a systematic way; instead, ad hoc reports, presentations, and spreadsheets are used. There is then difficulty in gaining a consistent or effective method of reporting progress and making comparisons across the portfolio. This typically becomes an issue after a couple of years of operating, as the business then asks for evidence of benefits. This issue is exacerbated if the team is dispersed globally and with different themes, technology, or business unit focus.

A systematic approach is needed to track and measure the following:

- **Contacts, initial assessments, and work flow.** This is important to save wasted effort across a team that could easily be looking at in excess of one thousand opportunities per annum. You also need to keep track of the history of engagement with a start-up, as the right time to invest has perhaps not arrived, although you need to be ready for the proper engagement. Keeping track is important, as the best start-up deals become competitive and you want to be ready for the right time to invest.

- **Due diligence and engagement with the start-up or partner.** This is an important phase, as this is when the majority of knowledge, insights, and relationships are built.

- **Investment details.** Investment details are key to understanding the performance of individual investments, with individual and team performance recognized.

- **Partnering and business unit engagement with the core business.** Understanding the opportunities and delivery of cost savings, new revenue, margins, and additional services is an important metric. It is difficult to attribute the benefits to venturing alone, but ensuring the solution is delivered and at scale is important.

- **Portfolio overview.** This is a key perspective that is often overlooked in innovation and venturing. When this happens, individual investments and portfolio financial returns may be discussed, but the connections between investments, the right mix of engagements, and investments in themes is not done effectively.

- **Innovative New Value Chain scenarios.** Organizations should be considering what scenarios are meetings people's needs in new ways by connecting technology, start-ups, and partners.

Being able to present the opportunities, with different perspectives, from teams globally, in real time is also an advantage. If you can collaborate with partners such as incubators and funds to increase the deal opportunities and insights, you will gain an advantage.

THE IMPORTANCE OF STRATEGIC ALIGNMENT

Gathering insights about technologies, business models, and geographies and transferring them into organizations in ways that are both sharable and actionable can be difficult to do in ways that are both methodical and measurable. Trying to make these gathered perspectives measurable is a key challenge.

Some organizations fall short by measuring the wrong performance indicators, asking questions about the number of meetings conducted, e-mails sent, or reports completed around a particular theme. Even Abdul Guefor of Intel Capital, quoted earlier, has admitted to falling into this trap in the past. That is, until he and his team realized that the softer measures yielded the true performance indicators—measures such as relationships formed and strategic insight gained. Intel, with its large team and billions of dollars invested, can track finances but puts great emphasis on the "softer" business unit feedback.

Looking to strategic insight and internal information sharing when measuring performance has other benefits that are, ironically, directly related to finance: gathering and applying insight within an organization leads to genuine and embedded learning that is far more cost-effective than hiring external consultants to produce research reports. In addition, these activities lower the acquisition costs associated with company expansions because better information breeds better decisions, and better decisions result in better bottom lines. Examples of engaging executives come in many forms and are dependent on both the industry and the culture of the organization. BP Castrol, for instance, has spoken about taking the executive team to new locations, such as the Meatpacking District in New York, and introducing them to Uber's CEO. This was before Uber had gotten to scale and caused disruption in the industry. You can easily imagine the corporate questioning the relevance of car sharing and not understanding this upstart venture. Now, we see the rise of the "gig economy" and peer-to-peer technology being applied in urban environments. Tony Askew of REV Venture Partners provided a strong example of the value of engaging for strategic insights.

Tony Askew, Founding Managing Partner of REV Venture Partners, described his views on strategic insight:

"We spend most of our time in profiling markets of interest, originating investment opportunities from our networks, negotiating and closing financing rounds, and sitting on boards and supporting our portfolio companies. Importantly, we also spend significant time, roughly 30 percent, working with RELX business units. Our investment activity, which involves reviewing thousands of early-stage companies a year, enables us to provide a complementary lens on the evolution of RELX business segments and interpret the impact of medium- and long-term technology trends on their businesses."[27]

To further illustrate this point, consider Jon Lauckner[28] of General Motors (GM) Ventures. While the GM corporation spends around $8 billion per annum on R&D[29] to create and improve vehicles, Lauckner's team believes it gains considerable insight into the marketplace from smaller-scale venture VC investments.

---

27 Tony Askew REV Venture Partners, July 16 –Video.

28 Jon Lauckner, GM, May 2015—Podcast Interview.

29 General Motors Company, *General Motors Annual Report* (2016), http://GM.com/ content/dam/gm/en_us/english/Group4/InvestorsPDFDocuments/10-K.pdf.

In an interview with Jon Lauckner,[30] I asked
how he measured the financial and strategic
performance of the CV investment.

Lauckner said, "The simple measure of our success is that the companies we invest in today have technology that winds up in the GM vehicles of tomorrow, generating greater sales and better profitability. Some technologies, particularly those that reduce cost or completely replace an incumbent technology, are easier to quantify in terms of their potential impact. However, we do not get overly fixated on trying to precisely quantify the strategic value of our portfolio because so-called superscoring models often require forecasting years into the future and to a level of precision not particularly useful or accurate. We typically evaluate financial value of our investments as the cash-on-cash return, although we have also looked at other return metrics."

ALIGNING TO GAIN INSIGHTS ACROSS HORIZONS

Performance measures vary across the Three Horizons of Purpose with respect to innovation. A corporation working in Horizon Three, for example, will be examining opportunities far removed from its core business model; therefore, the metrics it defines are likely going to be more strategic and insightful. A corporation working in Horizon One, on the other hand, will be engaging in activities close to its current business that provide an immediate cost benefit; therefore, the defined metrics will likely be financial in nature.

---

30 Jon Lauckner, GM, May 2015—Podcast Interview.

Organizations can bring together performance and portfolio management to have a repository of deal flow, diligence, and portfolio management. I have seen many organizations trying to do this in spreadsheets, document repositories, and intranets. These solutions do not, however, allow effective working across a geographically spread corporate venturing and innovation team that also has to engage with the business to validate and integrate effective working. Performance and portfolio solutions should therefore support the sharing of insights and delivery tracking of financial returns from the investment and impact in the business. Software as a service (SaaS) solutions, which teams can effectively use early in their innovation process, are now available for this.

In an article titled "Get Real! Are You Being Strategic or Tactical?"[31] I have argued that if your investment policy has too much "business unit" involvement in investment decision making, you are likely to be more tactical than strategic. There is often a debate within corporate venturing and open innovation units about whether they are strategic or financial—and whether the aim should be to be both.

---

31 Andrew Gaule, "Get Real! Are You Being Strategic or Tactical?" *Linkedin* (weblog), June 2016. https://www.linkedin.com/pulse/get-real-you-being-strategic-tactical-andrew-gaule.

KEY MESSAGES: PERFORMANCE, OPERATIONS, AND INSIGHTS

Performance measures for exploring and plotting the route to the future are difficult to identify. If you don't survive as a corporate, then you fail. And if you do not make a financial return as a corporate venturing unit, then you will not be making good deals and will not survive as a unit. It is not a matter of managing on financial or strategic measures alone but of managing both.

This book has moved through the 5Ps, discussing purpose, processes, partners, people, and performance. Setting metrics—that is, the performance stage—closes the loop on the 5Ps of corporate venturing.

Ultimately, corporates should approach the 5Ps as a comprehensive strategy for corporate venturing, and each part should be explored at the outset of any initiative. Focusing a disproportionate amount of time and resources on purpose and process, for example, can cause problems during the performance stage. Instead, corporate venturing strategies should be thorough and well rounded. When organizations understand this approach and have aligned the 5Ps, they can move on to driving even more growth by creating financial, strategic benefits and moving to industry-changing Innovative New Value Chains.

7. DRIVING THE INNOVATIVE NEW VALUE CHAIN

Do feel free to share!
@agaule

Organizations can align their strategic purpose while developing the process, partners, and people to deliver the performance. To be really strategic and of scale, they also need to be joining technologies, start-ups, and corporates to create Innovative New Value Chains. In this chapter, we will outline why the combination of technology and business models can now change the way we meet individuals' and businesses' needs. Corporate venturing and partnering can then be the way to move toward the more strategic opportunities the organization can address.

Making ad hoc investments aligned to the current business can be beneficial. If an organization invests this way and survives for more than three years in the world of corporate venturing, it is clearly making decisions that are tactically beneficial in terms of making returns. Simply looking at technologies or themes too closely aligned to the current business unit is not effective in the long term, however, to address the more disruptive areas that were outlined earlier.

Innovative New Value Chains are the result of orchestrated investments and allow corporate executives and those running their corporate venture and innovation units to be more strategic. To reach this point, though, these organizations must first overcome challenges surrounding the technology, start-ups, and corporates that will eventually align (see figure 7).

Bringing together technology, start-ups, and corporates has the potential to deliver new great opportunities. The application of new materials, devices in products, new payment methods, and increased social interaction with customers are coming together to change organizations and industries.

Innovative New Value Chains

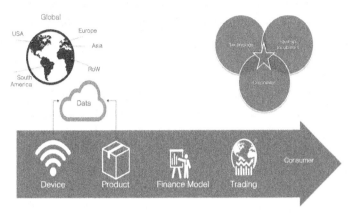

Figure 7

Today, there are several basic dysfunctions happening within the modern business and technology environment; these center on technology, start-ups, and corporates.

TECHNOLOGIES

As I have discussed, a large number of new technologies—from new materials, biotechnology, mobile devices, the Internet of things (IoT), big data, artificial intelligence, virtual and augmented reality, social media, and more—all continue to bring unmatched opportunities for organizations.

Simply deploying these or other new technologies into current products or services, however, does not ensure that these powerful tools are being used to their full potential. There is plenty of technology out there, but only a fraction of it is being deployed within current business models and that spells wasted opportunities for organizations. For an organization that truly prioritizes innovation, the question surrounding technology should not be merely how to scout and invest in it but how to change the model and scale it up.

As a "supermaterial," graphene has fantastic properties that were discovered and characterized at Manchester University in the United Kingdom. In an Innovative New Value Chain session at the Manchester University National Graphene Institute, leading experts and I explored the application of graphene. In current applications, graphene's properties of heat and electricity conductivity can be taken advantage of. It is being applied in rubber and concrete curing, which is cutting production time and providing additional features. Graphene is also being applied to composite materials, adding the advantages of strength and weight reduction, which significantly benefits high-performance automotive and aerospace applications.

The bigger potential, however, comes when its properties are applied to new devices and business models in health, transport, aerospace, electronics, and others, which then develop Innovative New Value Chains. Having functions for sensing and IoT connectivity at the microlevel opens up many opportunities that will require new processes and value opportunities.

START-UPS

Start-ups and incubators are important components of the ecosystem, and the marketplace is saturated with both. To complicate the matter, there are innovative initiatives being run by schools, universities, governments, corporates, venture capital companies, and more. Highlighted earlier were the 368 incubators and accelerators in the United Kingdom alone.[32] This is replicated—and at a greater scale—globally, with hot spots in Silicon Valley, Shanghai, Israel, and Europe. In my view, creating more is going to give lower returns and increased failures. Connecting and scaling effectively will give better financial and returns for the planet.

CORPORATES

Corporates, too, have challenges when it comes to

---

32 Jonathan Bone, Olivia Allen, and Christopher Haley, *Business Incubators and Accelerators: The National Picture* (London: Department for Business, Energy & Industrial Strategy, 2017).

making space for innovation, Horizon Three or otherwise. If modern organizations were more effective in their corporate venturing, open innovation, or venturing processes, they would have better opportunities. Finding those opportunities starts by understanding where corporates can add value. In organizations I have worked with, these tend to be in the realm of regulations, the management of assets, or the direct relationship with customers. For example, corporates can gain advantages from their understanding of regulations in clinical trials, the development of health solutions, transport, infrastructure, and financial services.

Ashok Vaswani, the chief executive of Barclays UK, has spoken about the value of corporate assets by saying his company is now a technology business with a balance sheet as it looks to deploy technologies out of its incubators and out of its banking business. Like many other corporates, Barclays is out to change business models and invest in technologies; its advantages lie in its assets and robust financials. The opportunity comes in identifying and deploying solutions.

ADDRESSING THE CHALLENGES

It is my provocative perspective that Silicon Valley has "done the easy stuff" by creating big businesses based on 140 characters on social media, computing centers focused on search algorithms, and disruptive technologies and business models (e.g., Uber and Airbnb) that mediate some current, long-standing channels or existing asset.

The bigger challenge today is deploying technologies that improve public health, transportation, and people's lives in general. To address these challenges, we will need to deploy technology and new business models in an environment that requires more asset investment, more engagement with people, and more regulation.

This task requires an environment familiar with regulations, yet committed to the care and delivery of technology as a solution, not simply a product or service. Innovative New Value Chains do just that, addressing the needs of consumers and the needs of society as a whole, rather than simply running software that bolsters current business models.

INNOVATIVE NEW VALUE CHAINS: WHAT THEY ARE NOT

Innovative New Value Chains are not Horizon One initiatives—that is, those that strive to make the current business model more efficient by producing alternative or adjacent products. Telecommunication company Vodafone, for example, ran some of its venture activities to find technologies that would be alternative-energy solutions for powering its base stations—a worthwhile cause, of course, because those activities build their core business. Just because those activities involve corporate venturing and technology, however, does not mean they represent the building of Innovative New Value Chains.

Innovative New Value Chains are also not *just* referring to the creation of new business models, which can also simply be called innovation. Consider Xerox and photo-copiers, for example. Xerox was not the first photocopier, but the business model of selling the photocopying capa-bilities on a price per print rather than selling a machine became an entirely new business model, and a successful one at that—just not an Innovative New Value Chain.

INNOVATIVE NEW VALUE CHAINS: WHAT THEY ARE

Innovative New Value Chains are not only new tech-nologies, new business models, or new start-up investments—they are formed from connecting the pieces of all three. Claudia Fan Munce, the retired founder of IBM Ventures, described in the foreword, "For me, the approach to innovation is to bring together the 'string of pearls' of technology and start-ups."

Innovative New Value Chains are relevant in a number of industries, and we will see examples of connecting technology and start-ups to give better outcomes in a number of scenarios. You will then see parallels with your organization and industry.

INNOVATIVE NEW VALUE CHAINS IN ACTION: AIMAVA AND MCLAREN APPLIED TECHNOLOGIES

McLaren Applied Technologies is an organization well known for several things: first, its Formula One business—the expertise surrounding the car, the race, and all the data in between. Second, McLaren also sells prestigious performance automobiles for off the racetrack. The third, less obvious arm of the business is McLaren Applied Technologies, a branch deeply vested in technology.

Geoff McGrath of McLaren Applied Technologies spoke on a panel I ran at the Global Corporate Venturing Symposium in London in May 2017.[33] We discussed the application of data and effective visualization to drive decisions and better outcomes for customers and business. In 2007, as an example of that application in action,

---

33 Andrew Gaule, "Making CVC Truly Strategic through Innovative New Value Chains," *LinkedIn* (blog), May 2017, https://www.linkedin.com/pulse/making-cvc-truly-strategic-through-innovative-new-value-andrew-gaule.

I worked with McLaren to develop a program around data capabilities. McLaren was able to capture data from vehicles and racetracks in locations such as Shanghai and Dubai and return it to London for analysis in a fraction of a second—giving the pit crew enough time to analyze and take action (e.g., bring a driver in for a pit stop). I helped them take that immense capability and consider how it could be applied to other industries, such as fast-moving consumer goods (FMCG), health, and transportation.

From this work, McLaren Applied Technologies partnered with National Air Traffic Services,[34] a group that manages air and ground traffic at the congested Heathrow Airport. The project centered on applying McLaren's rapid data analysis and visualization and turning these into actions to support transport infrastructure, transport networks, and other logistical areas both in and out of that sector.

Aimava has also led a program at McLaren Applied Technologies with a diabetes testing start-up, a health business, a FMCG business, a consumer business, a media company, and an industry-leading IoT technology infrastructure business. All the organizations came together to discuss Innovative New Value Chains, and during the program,

---

34 David Rowan, "Work Smarter: McLaren," *Wired*, March 1, 2010, http://www.wired.co.uk/article/work-smarter-mclaren.

we used the case of improving gestational diabetes testing for a particular group of people.

The basic model for gestational diabetes testing is as follows: a pregnant woman goes without food overnight, attends a clinic early the next day to have a blood test, consumes a glucose drink, takes another blood test after two hours, and waits for the results. The test is supposed to be taken by all expecting mothers, but the diabetes testing start-up found that fewer than 25 percent of women get tested in this way because women do not consider themselves ill, are busy with work or other childcare, and so on. The start-up had developed a solution to address this through an easy-to-use test women could take in their own homes, using technology to report the findings via a mobile device or easily delivering the data.

In the home test scenario, each player in the Innovative New Value Chain has different benefits and different challenges. During the workshop, for example, the health business representative said a challenge for her company was how to make more money by selling more tablets and devices to sick people—a key challenge of changing an existing business model. And although the solution would likely provide better patient outcomes and a better business process, it would be accompanied by a host of security and privacy hurdles—none of which would be insurmountable, but all of which need to be addressed by new players and approaches. In the case of the gestational diabetes test, the specific Innovative New Value Chain comprises the delivery of the device, the clinical test, the ability to capture data securely, and the ability to provide data feedback in terms of recommendations and results for patients.

The method and business model for payment may also change or shift to a different budget. However, many health start-ups are attempting to sell into the current health procurement process.

In another venture I supported—a smart bandage venture—members of the start-up commented that they felt procurement in health care was still working the same way it did in the days of Florence Nightingale (a nineteenth-century reformer and founder of "modern nursing"). That is, key players were not looking at how the new solution could provide more benefits and lower cumulative costs but were, rather, focused on the cheapest individual products (i.e., traditional bandages) in the current model of products and service.

Problems in the procurement process present a significant challenge, especially in the West. The implementation of new technology in China, though—explained thoroughly in chapter nine—creates an environment riper for innovation because innovators in that country are often willing to try new business models and technologies that deliver long-term value.

INNOVATIVE NEW VALUE CHAINS IN OTHER INDUSTRIES

Innovative New Value Chains apply to many other industries: agriculture, automotive, financial services, and more.

AGRICULTURE

Climate Corp, a Silicon Valley start-up developed by a former leader at Apple, was created around the concept of precision agriculture—that is, using data to identify the projected yield down to each square meter of land based on variable calculations including seed type, chemical usage, weather, and insurance. This information would be beneficial to individual farmers and agricultural businesses. Climate Corp had parts of the chain, but other players needed to create a true Innovative New Value Chain. An insurance company and an agricultural supply business did just that, and the result could mean much better outcomes for sustaining the agriculture industry, feeding the planet, and helping the environment. In

2013, Climate Corp was acquired by Monsanto for $930 million.[35]

AUTOMOTIVE

The automotive sector is undergoing significant change, with more data, diagnostics, electric vehicles, autonomy, and more. Castrol, the consumer brand and lubricants business of BP, has invested in in-car diagnostic businesses that monitor the way a vehicle is driven. Other businesses—insurance companies, for example—then invest as well because they are interested in that same technology. Castrol Ventures has also invested in businesses that can find trusted garages and service stations, as well as businesses that specialize in calendar upkeep and scheduling. Castrol Ventures presented what we call the Innovative New Value Chain at a Corporate Venturing Academy I led in May 2017, demonstrating the end result: the system would know if a vehicle had been driven differently than normal, know the nearest and most trusted repair shop, know whether that business has the capacity to service the vehicle that week, and know whether the owner of the vehicle will not be needing the vehicle at that time (e.g., if they will be out of the country). Creating

---

35 Bruce Upbin, "Monsanto Buys Climate Corp for $930 Million," *Forbes*, October 2, 2013, http://forbes.com/sites/bruceupbin/2013/10/02/monsanto-buys-climate-corp-for-930-million/#6e1b75b1177a.

a system that has this knowledge can remove the need for the customer to realize the need for service, take the effort to arrange it, and manage their schedule so that the car is not needed for a day. Additional efficiencies in capacity management also give more benefits. This is a simple automotive example that gets even more interesting and challenging when we have autonomous electric vehicles, which act as energy storage devices and that are often shared. Determining which technology and business model is then required is a challenge many start-ups and incumbents in the industry are now exploring.

ENERGY UTILITY

A primary example of this concept in action is Nest, a California start-up acquired in 2014 by Google for $3.2 billion. Nest's key product was originally a smart home thermostat. Fundamentally, though, its product has always been a platform for capturing data from the increasing number of connected devices in homes. When a utility company began to deploy the technology, possibilities increased exponentially.

Prior to deploying the Nest platform, utility companies sold a commodity: electricity. After the shift, though, the utility works as a conduit for a technology that can actively manage efficiencies in new and valuable ways, from electricity to heating to alternative-energy generation. It is precisely this type of organizational context—open to possibility and highly strategic—that is the foundation for Innovative New Value Chains.

HEALTH SERVICES

Merck in the United States (and known as MSD in the rest of the world) is a global health business dealing with prescription products, oncology, and animal health. Bill Taranto leads Merck's Global Health Innovation Fund as part of the larger Merck ecosystem dedicated to innovation. Taranto and his team are focused on connected health, combining emerging information tools with existing health data to improve the quality of health outcomes at lower health costs. In a recent interview, Taranto described the objective of the business, and it is an excellent example of an Innovative New Value Chain development. I think this is such a good case that I have included a significant portion of the interview[36] here.

---

36 William (Bill) Taranto, Merck, May 2017—Podcast Interview.

Interview with Bill Taranto of Merck's Global Health Innovation Fund, May 2017

Gaule: Could we kick off with a brief introduction to the Global Health Innovation Fund and to Merck?

Taranto: I am head of Merck's Global Health Innovation Fund. I joined Merck—it will be actually seven years this April—to start their VC activities. They had not actually done any VC work prior to that.

Prior to joining Merck, I was at Johnson & Johnson [J & J] for close to twenty years, and spent the majority of my career investing for them as well.

Today, we are a $500 million fund and have over thirty-five portfolio companies. We have had about seven exits to date, and Merck's actually acquired two of our companies to date, so we think we are delivering what Merck asked us to on day one—that is, to try to give Merck a number of options around this non-core area of health care.

Gaule: Can you give us some examples of what "Connected Health" means to Merck and your fund?

Taranto: One of the most important things that I think a venture fund needs to do is have a strategy—especially a corporate venture fund. So, when you say you are investing on behalf of the core, that is not actually a strategy but is really more about a broad tactic. And when I would say, "I am investing not on behalf of the core," that is not really a strategy. I think one of the most fundamental mistakes a corporate venture firm makes is not having a well-defined strategy.

The way we think of our strategy—and health care very uniquely is positioned to have this type of strategy in that what happens in health care versus other industries is hard to scale because of the local and regional nature by which health care is practiced—is to build it around how we are going to invest and how we are actually going to scale. Then, we bring that value back to the parent company.

We created this thing called Connected Health. The way to think about it is operating on two fundamental investment theses. And this is, again, only related to health care. Our first investment thesis is that we believe data is the currency we are going to use for transactions in the future market. What does that mean? It means that we want all our companies to touch data in some way. Whether they are aggregating data, analyzing data, throwing off data like a diagnostic test or a monitoring company, that they all touch data in a certain way. Because health care is based on value and outcomes, data is what drives that value and outcome. That is our first fundamental investment thesis.

The second is that one of the big lessons I learned from all the years investing at J & J, in health care specifically, is that point solutions do not work. And a point solution is a very narrow company focused on a very narrow widget, if you will. The problem with health care is that it is much broader than that. So, we work in what we call an interconnected health-care framework. What we try and do is connect companies. By that I mean when we look at an investment company, if we cannot connect it to another company within our portfolio or outside of our portfolio, we do not do that investment. We are trying to make sure that we can partner this company. Partnering can mean a lot of things—it can mean actually merging them together, or it can be a commercial agreement, or it can just be a handshake that we are going to try to work together and deliver an integrated solution to the market.

The way we think about it in health care is that existing data tools exist today. There is existing data that is commodity data—things like electronic medical records and data of patients' health care. Everybody has access to the data; you can actually buy this data.

The problem is that existing data does not tell you a lot about a specific patient. We are really interested in investing in what we call emerging informational tools, which can be things like point-of-care diagnostic companies, molecular diagnostic companies, or remote monitoring companies. It could involve mobile and social. It encompasses all this new data that is being generated by these companies. Now, our goal is to merge this new data with commodity data, and you create what is called a large patient data set—one that is much deeper and allows us to know more about a patient than we knew before.

That's just the beginning. What is really important for us is the next step, which is investing in the middle layer: health IT platforms. Why is that important? The problem is if you cannot aggregate data, integrate data, and harmonize data, you cannot actually use the data that you are collecting. What we want, then, is to make sure we have an infrastructure layer that allows us to do three main things. One is to secure data in a private setting so it would be HIPAA compliant [the 1996 Health Insurance Portability and Accountability Act (HIPAA) requires confidential handling of protected health information].

Two is to aggregate, integrate, and harmonize that data. Third, we want to analyze that data. We are interested in companies that can do all those types of things. Here's the problem: You cannot get to a solution in the end if you just have disparate data and you do not have it infrastructurally.

We want to make sure we are collecting new data and are providing the middle layer to house that data to make it usable to get to the upper layer—that is, the place where all the solutions occur. The upper layer includes precision medicine or diagnostic companies. It could also be monitoring companies that allow you to have the right patient, right place, right time sort of concept.

We are also very interested in clinical awareness and decision support tools and how we get them to work well in practicing medicine. In addition, we are interested in quality and performance improvements—that is, how you go into a hospital system and remove costs and create better efficiencies—things like care coordination and infection control. If I were very interested in the provider of patient engagement, how do you actually talk to the physician and talk to the patient and how do they talk together? You can actually bring better quality information to all the right parties.

All this works together because if you just do investments in any one of these small buckets, that is a point evolution. If you do investments in these buckets and connect them to other buckets, that is the integrated health-care framework that we work in. So again, what we try to do is follow our investment theses: data is the currency, make sure it is a data company, and make sure we can connect it to another company.

Gaule: I am seeing the points you are making here in other sectors: automotive, utility, consumer, agriculture. Automotive now is not about a metal box on rubber wheels with some electronics in it; it is about autonomous vehicles, data, car sharing, that whole value chain and ecosystem. As you have illustrated here in terms of health, I think it is applicable to other sectors.

Taranto: I agree 100 percent. You call it Innovative New Value Chain; we call it ecosystem investing. I will cover it later, but it is the most important foundation of what we do. I agree with you; I am starting to see in all other industries where point solutions are not working, that you actually have to work in this sort of value chain or ecosystem and bring companies together to bring a much more holistic or engaged solution to the market. They cannot seem to get where they want to go with point solution answers.

Gaule: In a number of corporates, a number of sectors I have touched on, corporates need to string together different technologies, different start-ups, in what I term Innovative New Value Chain, where the business model is going to change and where an industry or sector might change. When we were at the GCV Academy in New York, I described a program that we did at McLaren where we brought together a diabetes testing business and fast-moving consumer goods businesses and pharmaceutical businesses to look at how that Innovative New Value Chain changed.

You then talked about your ecosystem structure. Could you talk it through and give us one of the examples?

Taranto: When we think in terms of the integrated health-care system that we like to invest in, we created something called ecosystem investing. How it works in health care for us is we actually do not start with a company, but we actually start with what we call a use case or a customer need. What we try to do first is try to understand what is happening and how can we solve that problem for the end user. We start with something that in health care it is called a use case, but it is really just solving a problem in health care. It might be trying to deliver better care, talking about lowering costs, or just delivering health care more effectively and more conveniently—but's always about solving a problem.

The big thing about health care that is a little different, too, as we think about these problems is it is not really about solving a technology problem. It is about solving a health-care problem utilizing technology. Technology is an enabler. That is why we do not really start with the company first; we actually start with the problem.

Once we have identified the problem, we try to identify what we call an anchor tenant. The anchor tenant, much like a mall, is the store, if you will, that draws everybody in. It is a company that can solve typically anywhere from 50 percent to 60 percent of the use case, or the problem, that you are trying to solve. It never solves 100 percent. Those companies are not easily findable and really do not exist, so we try to find somebody that can actually solve a lot of the issues that we are trying to solve.

From that, it's much like how a mall is built. We put stores around it, so we invest around it to fill the gaps. That is how the ecosystem is beginning to get built. You can almost say that the anchor tenant is your sun, and the planets around it are your areas of which you are trying to fill all the gaps of that particular need.

Then, what we try to do over time, is to connect these companies and have them work together. They can work together in many different ways. We are trying to leverage the key strengths that these companies have. The collaboration can just be a vendor relationship, as I mentioned before. It could be a joint venture or go-to-market sort of agreement. It can be a platform collaboration. It can be a merger where you bring the companies together. But the whole idea is, over time, by building this ecosystem, it allows us to build bigger scale so should Merck want to partake in whatever that use case is solving, it is easier for them to do it by aggregating companies together and bringing a much more integrated solution to the market versus that point solution. What that scale then does for Merck or any parent is it drives a better relationship with the customer you are trying to help, but it also drives revenue and EPS [earnings per share]. Why? Because when you build a bigger solution that takes care of a wider net of end users, you have a better ability to drive what you are trying to do for your parent. Again, for us, it was around driving revenue and EPS ultimately in the company.

We call it roll-up. How do you move to a roll-up? You might start with just a company or companies with handshakes or some kind of commercial agreement, but the whole idea over time is to figure out which companies best work together within that ecosystem. It may not be all the ones you've invested in within that ecosystem, though; you might have six companies in an ecosystem and four of them are the ones that could deliver the best solution together. Then, we'd bring them together.

A perfect example of how we have actually done this is we have created an ecosystem around remote care monitoring in the cardiac space. We started with a venture investment, which we called our anchor tenant, in a company called Preventice—but, of course, it actually started with a use case. The use case in this particular instance was the high prevalence of AFib, or atrial fibrillation, which many people have. It's the fluttering of the heart which can lead to things like a stroke or a heart attack. The question was: How do we actually solve it?

That condition was what was causing many to see thirty-day read-missions into the hospital program—that is, where a patient gets discharged, but they end up back in the hospital because they cannot control this AFib. We invested in this little company called Preventice. What Preventice was doing was just the front end of the monitoring. They had a patch that looked like a band-aid that could actually do full AFib in a closed-loop system. They could actually take the reads of the device. Our partner in this particular instance was Mayo, and they would send that data back to the Mayo cardiology lab where they would read them. Then, they'd get back to the patient and manage the patient.

What we found was that Preventice only was the front end. It was just the patch. We actually did not have any back end. How do you handle a call center? Who's actually doing the readings? How do you clean the devices and get all of the different devices out of the patient? How do you handle reimbursing? We identified a company called eCardio and decided to have them begin to work together in a commercial partnership. We found that their commercial partnership worked so well, where Preventice was providing the front end (the actual device) and eCardio was providing the back end (the actual physical monitoring) that we decided to roll them up and bring them together into an integrated solution—one where we had the ability to offer both the front end and the back end in a single entity.

One of the pieces we were missing, though, was the care coordination component. How do you actually care for the patient if they are on this device? We acquired a third company called C3 Nexus, a care coordination company around the thirty-day readmit in the cardio-vascular program. They have nurse programs, contact the patient, and walk them through how to both use the device and manage their condition. It's a full care coordination program. Interestingly, by bringing those three pieces together, we are a better solution for anybody that wants to do cardio monitoring because we had the front end, the back end, and the care coordination component.

As we (Merck), through our private equity fund, consolidated all three companies together, we realized that Merck actually is not a cardiovascular company. It is not one of our therapeutic specialties. So, we deconsolidated our position and brought in Boston Scientific as our lead partner—them being both a device company and a cardiovascular company. That relationship has been going fantastic since then, and we have built what we consider one of the best-in-class, top cardiovascular monitoring companies in the country. But it was all done through identifying this ecosystem around a problem, first and foremost. We asked what companies could help that problem and how we could bring them together through investing. Then, we did.

Gaule: Are you able to share the financial benefits of using the approach you have described here?

Taranto: In the case of the Preventice-eCardio deal, when we ended up deconsolidating our position, because we had created such value, we paid Merck back all the money we had previously invested. Corporates can add better value—they are one of the few entities that have the ability to do this aggregation of assets. Typically, private venture firms do not have the ability to do that, and certainly private equity firms do, but we have more expertise within our own industry and actually make a better partner to these companies than private equity, because we have skin in the game, we are in health care as a vendor.

But generally speaking for our fund, we are measured in a couple of different ways. From a financial perspective, Merck did not hire me to lose money—they would like us to provide a return and be evergreen. The important thing for us is that we do not ever have to go back for Merck to replenish the $500 million. The idea is to be self-sufficient and Merck allows us to keep any gains on sales of assets, and then we just replenish the fund and keep moving forward and keep adapting our strategy.

From the strategic side, are we doing what Merck asked us to do? Are we giving them option on their M&A [mergers and acquisitions]? Are we giving them assets that they believe are viable? If we are not providing them those assets, then we are not investing in the right way. Fortunately for us, they have acquired a number of our companies, so we continue to build value. As long as we have built a good investment and a good health-care company, we can exit that, then reinvest in places that Merck might find more attractive over the next few years.

Gaule: This is a fantastic example of Innovative New Value Chains because you are focusing on need rather than just doing point investments. You see what is happening in the marketplace, you see the technologies, you see the business model, and you are the one who will orchestrate bringing together the partnership and the relationship.

FINANCIAL SERVICES

The financial services sector is undergoing considerable technology and business model change as mobile devices and electronic transactions are becoming easier. Technology businesses are becoming the financial intermediaries with the likes of Apple Pay. Also, potentially more disruptive are the payment, credit, and savings solutions implemented by the Chinese financial services business Ant Financials, which is associated with Alibaba, the retail and IT business.

In 2013, another Chinese solution, WeChat, implemented mobile payments embedded in the social and transaction platform of Tencent. In 2014, they launched a clever marketing and social interaction campaign based on the traditional red envelope given at Chinese New Year. Over the Chinese New Year period, the number of people on the payment platform increased from 30 million to more than 100 million. At an academy I was running in Shanghai in 2016, Jeffrey Li (who leads the Tencent

Venture Fund) described the rapid rise of users on the platform (now more than 900 million active users) and payment penetration in a high proportion of these users. The growth and penetration are continuing at a fast pace. In fact, at some shops and food malls in China in April 2017, I could not make a purchase without a WeChat, Alipay, or some temporary card. It's clear the Innovative New Value Chain is occurring with new devices, payment technology, and interaction.

The insurance sector is also looking for new value and transaction opportunities in automotive, health, and asset insurance. I asked Jacqueline LeSage Krause[37] of Munich RE Ventures, "Are you seeing new products, services, and business models that are brought together in different ways to the current business—what I would term Innovative New Value Chains?" She replied, "Absolutely. That has been especially true over the past five to ten years for telematics and other sensor-based technologies that can be integrated into insurance in either light form or very disruptive ways."

Financial services are also going to be disrupted by blockchain transaction technologies and following the flow of value in an Innovative New Value Chain is going to become very different from the payment for product or

37 Jacqueline LeSage Krause, Munich RE Ventures, Jan. 2016—Podcast Interview.

services. We do not at the moment know how or where these changes are going to occur—that is why you need to be in the ecosystem looking at technology, start-ups, and business models.

CREATING AND CAPTURING VALUE

Value must be created and captured within an Innovative New Value Chain, and getting there can be challenging. In a corporate round table discussion, one organization described the value areas in Innovative New Value Chain as being akin to dumbbells. In their view, a successful corporate venturing initiative has got to either have robust technologies with proven outcomes (not just projections or trials) or, at the other end of the Innovative New Value Chain, strong customer relationships.

Apple, for example, has strong relationships with its customer base, so it can string together technologies to create substantial value in the brand. There could also be value along that chain if a corporation brings capabilities and assets—for example, if a corporation has the logistics and supply chain to deliver an excellent customer experience or the regulatory experience necessary to manage a business in a different industry, such as finance.

Intellectual property (IP) is an important component of

the discussion around capturing value. Ian Harvey, who was CEO of BTG (British Technology Group) and is a member of Aimava's advisory panel, is passionate about this issue. Harvey has experience in intellectual assets and identifying value that allow corporates the space to develop, protect, and exploit value via avenues such as trademarks and patents. Know-how is critical here; how an organization orchestrates the knowledge it has about what is going on within and outside of its ecosystem—the funds, the technologies—is crucial for developing Innovative New Value Chains. The connection to China is also seen as important for Harvey, as he has seen the rise of China in IP management and building, an understanding that has led to the creation of the IP program at Tsinghua University in Beijing.

The Industrial Revolution was built around the intellectual property of Watt, Tesla, Westinghouse, and many others. But today, many CEOs and C-suite executives miss the relevance of intellectual property (IP), which underpins 70 to 80 percent of the value of most companies.

—IAN HARVEY[38]

That know-how for Innovative New Value Chain creation is generally held within the strategic innovation and cor-

---

38 From the foreword of this book.

porate venturing group. If matters are handled properly, the venturing group has seen the deals and the technologies—an intellectual asset capability in and of itself.

ORCHESTRATING GLOBALLY

Innovative New Value Chains need to include capabilities from different locations—where an organization invests, how it connects, how it partners, and how it chooses to consolidate them all are important areas, and companies such as Merck, GE, and IBM strive on all fronts.

Other organizations, however, are still coming to this awareness. At the conclusion of a two-day academy in Silicon Valley, for example, one corporate venturing leader from an aerospace company realized the value of scale in Innovative New Value Chains and indicated his company was missing an $18 billion opportunity.

When it comes to succeeding with Innovative New Value Chains, scale is best discussed at the global level. Whereas start-ups are typically in only one location and backed by local funding, corporates are in the position to gather vision from European markets, leverage the technological capabilities of Silicon Valley, and leverage the manufacturing leadership of China to launch globally. We will consider the global aspect shortly, in chapter nine.

KEY MESSAGES

Industries are being fundamentally changed as technologies and start-ups are coming together to deliver new products and solutions. The car industry, for example, is no longer about metal boxes on rubber wheels. Cars are now made from composite smart materials that can capture energy from the sun and store it for off-grid energy, have the computing power to be autonomous, and can be shared in a congested urban environment. Which industries are being disrupted and who will capture the value now?

Participating in Innovative New Value Chains gives an organization the chance to become truly strategic, making corporate venturing beneficial for the company and serving as a potential catalyst for societal change. Companies need to create and sustain Innovative New Value Chains by doing the following:

- Understanding the investment ecosystem

- Scouting and investing in start-ups and the new VC opportunities they create

- Orchestrating new business models

8. KEEPING IT LEGAL

This chapter does not provide legal advice. It does, however, highlight common legal considerations of organizations involved in corporate venturing. Be sure to get the appropriate advice from experts in the regions you are doing your deals.

Large corporates have robust legal departments, and those legal departments are often familiar with partnering with suppliers, commissioning services, engaging in mergers and acquisitions, and more. What they are *not* generally familiar with are the issues that are critical to corporate venturing, such as looking at budding technologies, partnering with start-ups, and making early investments, often alongside venture capital (VC) investors.

The legalities around corporate venturing differ from the legalities in day-to-day operations of large parent organizations for two key reasons. First, they involve smaller investment amounts of typically between $100,000 and $10 million, as outlined in the model for corporate venture capital (CVC). These minority stake activities are vastly different from billion-dollar acquisitions or starting new divisions, activities with which many *Fortune* 500 companies are familiar.

Second, in the context of CVC, corporates are usually investing to take less than 20 percent of the start-up, as this puts the investment below a level where it needs to be consolidated to the corporate accounts. This saves a lot in the way of accounting and declaration for the start-up CVC unit and work for the finance department of the corporate parent. This minority stake is also below a level considered to have control, which can provide protection for liabilities.

In-house legal counsel is often unprepared to offer the advice and support for smaller investments because its priority is, of course, to work on more immediate and much larger deals. Proceeding with in-house counsel is a waste of the corporate parents' resources, and it is also a source of frustration for small start-ups that can often feel smothered by large legal departments.

Corporate venturing requires early-stage investments that necessitate ongoing relationships with start-ups as those businesses are further developed. The early-stage investment and ongoing relationship can be spoiled if an inappropriate agreement is imposed on the smaller start-up—which, remember, is not versed in corporate legal speak—by the larger organization.

BrainJuicer (now called System1 Group) was one of the first early-stage investments made by Unilever Ventures in 2002. BrainJuicer listed on the London AIM Stock Exchange in 2006. The founding chief executive has spoken about how the initial discussions and terms were coming from the corporate legal department more suited to a large acquisition than a start-up. This relationship and investment was a success, but it is an example of an aspect of start-up and corporate investment that caused frustration in the early stage of the relationship.

LEGAL ASPECTS OF CORPORATE VENTURING

There are several legal aspects that must be considered in the world of CV; these include term sheets for making an investment, intellectual property (IP), and board memberships.

TERM SHEETS

A term sheet is a document outlining the principal economic and control terms of a proposed investment. It is usually nonbinding but may have some legal or reputational obligations on the investor and the company.

There are template term sheets available from the National Venture Capital Association[39] (NVCA) in the United States and the British Venture Capital Association[40] (BVCA) in the United Kingdom. Typical start-up and ecosystem venture capital communities have standard templates within regions. The valuations and detail entered into a term sheet of course vary as a result of geography, industry, market conditions, founders, and investor requirements. The numbers and details may differ, but the concepts remain the same. Term sheets cover a variety of information, including the following:

---

39 "Model Legal Documents," *National Venture Capital Association*, http://nvca.org/resources/model-legal-documents/.

40 "Model Documents for Early-stage Investments," *British Private Equity & Venture Capital Association*, https://www.bvca.co.uk/Policy/Tax-Legal-and-Regulatory/Industry-guidance-standardised-documents/Model-documents-for-early-stage-investments.

- **The economics of deals**, including details such as what percentage of equity was sold for what price and what the parameters are for warranties or future deals.

- **Details about control mechanisms**, that is, who will fill board seats, who will have rights for voting or vetoing future rounds of funding, and more.

- **Valuation controls**, or protections and preferences so the investors are covered if there is a down round of funding or when the business floats.

- **Opportunities around managing liquidity**, or the ability of organizations to retrieve money if they choose not to follow on with the investment.

- **Options for exiting deals**, including providing specific information about how and when investing bodies can leave deals while gaining the financial returns on their investments.

To accompany this book, there is a glossary of terms.[41] Terms and the process of investment are also covered further in the book *Venture Deals: Be Smarter Than Your Lawyer and Venture Capitalist* by Brad Feld and Jason Mendelson.

---

41 Find the glossary at Aimava.com/resources.

VCs and other investors will be wary of investing alongside a corporation that is expecting special terms in term sheets. This concept can often be difficult for a corporation to understand and accept, but it is a lesson echoed by many who have been involved in local investment ecosystems. Including terms of rights of first refusal, exclusivity, conditions on other investors, or exit conditions can stop a deal, as they limit the options on bidders or exits for a venture, which, of course, lowers the potential financial rewards. As very few exits are to the investing corporate—some figures say around 5 percent—the vast majority of the time, the corporate investor is the seller. So, it's in the corporate investor's best interest to get the best price. With special terms, corporates will not be considered to join a deal. If a start-up and other investors are willing to accept special terms, you have to question whether it is likely to be a good deal or whether you are the "dumb money."

It is also important to recognize that an early-stage investment is the start of a long-term relationship with the venture. There will be ups and down as technology, market, and team challenges occur. Follow-on investments will be required as the venture reaches, or misses, its milestones for the next stage of development.

I have found that taking corporate cross-functional teams

through a real VC case study and making decisions on investments, role playing on a board, going through further investment rounds, changing team members, and bringing on board new investors helps to align the understanding and experiences of participants. It is important to allow some of the capability development to happen in a safe environment rather than learning on the job with real companies and millions of dollars of investment.

INTELLECTUAL PROPERTY

IP is an important factor that must be considered during corporate venturing. Corporates must conduct due diligence around which company or entity owns the IP and assets of the start-up being supported. For example, sometimes IP can be owned by the company being invested in, the founder of the start-up who might be registered as the patent owner, or another person or organization. Ownership can be more complicated to determine in some instances than others. Contracts should clearly state that the IP is owned by the company and not by the creator or the contractor who did the work.

Just as rights for IP ownership can differ, so can those for development. If a company invests in a start-up that plans to continue to develop technologies in a niche area that interests the corporation, who has rights to the IP as it develops? Questions like this must be addressed at the outset of the investment process.

Inherent to the landscape of corporate venturing is the danger of the contamination or crossover of IP. To avoid such a damaging scenario, investors must take care to differentiate between their rights as investors and their rights within joint development agreements made around areas such as R&D, production, or sales. The differentiation here is important because those individuals working on investment corporate venture deals are not necessarily the appropriate people to be working on IP rights deals in terms of joint development. Keeping the terms of the investment separate from joint development agreements is seen as being the most appropriate approach. It removes complexity in the share agreements and maintains the distinction on the roles and responsibilities in the deal.

Tim Smith of Rouse, a global IP consultancy firm, has often spoken about IP pitfalls, particularly related to working with start-ups and various funds within China, a rapidly changing region. Smith has provided an overview of the key types of IP, the IP issues related to investing and developing, and specific areas to consider in China.[42]

It is important to understand that Chinese rights and

42 Tim Smith, Rouse, Nov. 2016—Video Interview.

protections are strengthening, as China is developing its own IP and is therefore putting robust and effective systems into it. In a report written by Ian Harvey in 2014,[43] he highlighted the following:

The role of IP and its enforcement in China is much more advanced than most people realize:

1. IP law in China is of a high quality by global standards.

2. The quality, cost and timeliness of the "rights" (patents and trademarks) granted to foreign firms under Chinese law compare well with the rest of the world.

3. Enforcement of patent rights is much cheaper and faster than in most developed countries. The courts, including the IP Tribunal of the Supreme Court, are handing down some very sophisticated judgements. The ability to enforce varies in different localities in China.

---

43 Ian Harvey, *Intellectual Property: China in the Global Economy—Myth and Reality* (report, 2014). Ian Harvey was CEO of BTG plc from 1985 until his retirement in late 2004. He was chairman of the UK Intellectual Property Institute from 1999 to 2011. He is currently chairman of the IP Center Advisory Board, Tsinghua University x-lab, Beijing.

Neil Foster of Baker Botts has provided valuable perspectives on information protocols and agreements that corporate investors can put in place to make sure IP rights are fair and explicit. This becomes especially important when corporates have nominated board or observer seats, which means they have access to information.

SITTING ON A BOARD

When a corporate invests in a start-up, it makes decisions as to how it will approach seating members on the board of that start-up. For example, it can invest only and not take or be given board seats, invest and choose to seat personnel on the board as observers only, or invest and seat board members with full duties. There are several considerations associated with the last two options. This distinction is important because those new to corporate venturing may enter agreements as either representatives of their parent corporates or as individuals of their parent corporates without understanding the difference between the roles.

While board observers do not have the fiduciary duties of being full board members, these positions still require legal agreements to clarify rights and obligations for everyone involved in information rights—the board observers, the start-ups, and other investors.

Full board members are individually responsible and liable. When I lead training programs, in fact, I often find that individuals quickly turn to their legal departments to look for independent legal advice.

A fiduciary duty is an obligation to act in the best interest of another party, such as a start-up company. A person acting in a fiduciary capacity is held to a high standard of honesty and full disclosure.

While observers on boards of start-ups do not have fiduciary duties, they do have legal responsibilities to act within the terms of the agreements. As observers, though, these individuals are not directors or officers and therefore are not granted the ability to get director and officer (D&O) insurance coverage. It could also be shown that if responsibilities and actions are not appropriately taken, such an individual could be seen as shadow director.

A number of CVCs express the view that if a corporate is going to invest time, resources, and finances to sit on the board of a start-up, it is best to do so properly, by sitting on that board personally, after getting legal advice. Board members must understand the factors at play and always act in good faith. Besides satisfying legal obligations, having all these boxes checked often better enables corporates to provide value to the start-up and ultimately see a return on that investment.

This recommendation to fully sit on the board is also based on the fact that people are at the heart of the 5Ps of corporate venturing, and boards are ultimately a group of people working toward the same goal. Sitting at a table monthly or quarterly with other experts and investors is an important process, and not coming at it fully committed or with the appropriate agenda can put a board member in a difficult position. Legally, board members must act in the best interest of the start-up company, not their employers or shareholders.

Granted, others at the table will have their own interests. The founder of the start-up, for example, is an employee, a shareholder, and a director, each of which comes with its own agenda and potential conflicts. Financial investors, too, have objectives to invest in the start-up, help it grow, then exit that business at the time of maturity. As corporate investors, the goals are to encourage the start-up while also gaining broader information about technology and trends that will inform the future of the marketplace.

It was very informative to hear John Kearon, in a video case study,[44] discuss how he developed BrainJuicer and

---

44 John Kearon, BrainJuicer, Nov. 2016—Video Interview.

how it went through investment and growth with Unilever Ventures, as well his handling of his role on the board. The perspectives on the exit to IPO were also particularly interesting, as there were differing views of board and shareholders.

It is important to reiterate shareholders and corporate investors do not have the rights to all information in the company, but board members have rights and responsibilities around that information. Knowing what information and insight can be divulged and what must be kept within the walls of the boardroom must be outlined in information protocols to make this clear for all participants. Having a dedicated corporate venturing unit can help because it has embedded roles and responsibilities with some separation from the corporate parent, allowing board members who hail from the venturing unit to differentiate between their roles and providing an important level of separation from the core business.

Mark Radcliffe[45] of DLA Piper, too, has given presentations at a number of my corporate venturing academies that provided extensive background and context on term sheets, IP issues, and the complexities of sitting on a board. Radcliffe has also developed online training material

---

45 Mark Radcliffe, DLA Piper, Jul. 2015—Video Interview.

on the board roles, which can be a valuable resource to executives taking up the role.

KEY MESSAGE

When a corporate goes through the process of investing in a minority stake in a start-up, it gains benefits of insights from being in the flow of thousands of deals and an understanding of the dynamics involved in leading start-ups. Being an investor and board member of a venture has legal implications and responsibilities for the success of the business. The executives and companies that I believe do a good job in corporate venturing recognize they need to work first and foremost in the interest of the start-up and *then* look after the corporate interests. You will not have any great insights or a financial return if the venture fails. As we have seen, being an investor and being on the board of a start-up is very different from a typical corporate role. Corporates active within the start-ups in which they have invested are privy to a new level of strategic insight they can then apply to assist in making a larger return within that start-up and their core business. Managing the differences is critical to the success of corporate venturing.

9. GLOBAL INNOVATION SUPERPOWERS

Do feel free to share! @agaule

There are many geographic centers of innovation throughout the world that impact global corporate venturing players. The purpose of this book is not to go into detail about each region and its funds, start-ups, and ecosystem. I do, however, want to highlight the global nature of innovation and some of the dynamics to be considered. Venture capital funds and individual start-ups tend to be geographically focused on a particular area of expertise or a solid developmental ecosystem. Strategically combining start-ups with technologies and corporates often requires operation on a global scale. Corporates must understand where the innovation hot spots are related to their industries and use that information to bring together the components of Innovative New Value Chains.

Different global centers have different areas of expertise and we are going to have an opportunity to touch on only a very few. Over a number of decades, Silicon Valley has created a strong technology ecosystem that was built on early government defense spending. This has been enhanced by a robust venture capital community—high net worth angel investors with scale-up experience, who are able to finance the plethora of start-ups flocking to the area. In fact, even though many start-ups may begin elsewhere around the world, many move to Silicon Valley because they know they can get the funding and support they need to grow. As a result of the start-up surplus, successful corporate venturing units often scout in this area.

While certainly powerful, Silicon Valley is not the only location ripe for innovation. The East Coast of the United States, for example, tends to be a hotbed for health innovation, including pharmaceutical discoveries and next-generation genomics. While many understand the scale and capabilities of the United States, many new other hot spots are arising.

Israel is an interesting and strong ecosystem in many areas, including technology, data security, health applications, and new materials. I am grateful to Yoni Dolgin of UK Israel Tech Hub for sharing his perspectives with me on the reasons for and scale of the innovation system in Israel. The ecosystem has been built on a close community made stronger by the involvement of many in the military. Thus, key players have experience with advanced problem solving and working with high-technology solutions. In addition, active government and private sector development has been a catalyst for the VC and technology incubator infrastructure.

One of the corporate incubators and investors in Israel and the key regions is Microsoft. You can learn more about the ecosystem in my interviews with Zack Weisfeld[46] of Microsoft Accelerators and Nagraj Kashyap[47] of Microsoft Ventures.

I have also run programs in Russia, which is strong in physical science, material sciences, and cybersecurity. China, too, has very quickly developed its capabilities, and I think the country is in a unique position because that innovation is scalable thanks to a growing economy and expanding infrastructure.

---

46 Zack Weisfeld, Microsoft Accelerators, Nov. 2016—Podcast Interview.

47 Nagraj Kashyap, Microsoft Ventures, Oct. 2016—Podcast Interview.

CHINA TAKING THE LEAD

China is a specific example of a global innovation super-power that deserves a deeper discussion. Since 1978, when Deng Xiaoping opened the economy and gave the region its economic drive, growth has been exponential and led by its government's five-year plans. From my travels and business in China over thirteen years, it has certainly struck me that the country has a strategic plan and is very pragmatic and focused on achieving its objectives. At one of my events, a Chinese observer of business and politics said the leaders in China are highly experienced and delivery-oriented. At the time, seven out of the nine most prominent leaders in China were engineers who had previously run significant government departments and large state-owned enterprises.

China is now on its thirteenth five-year plan, and innovation is at the top of the list of high-level process areas that fortify the strategies outlined:

- **Innovation:** Move up in the value chain by abandoning old, heavy industry and building up bases of modern information-intensive infrastructure.

- **Balancing:** Bridge the welfare gaps between countryside and cities by distributing and managing resources more efficiently.

- **Greening:** Develop the environmental technology industry, as well as ecological living and ecological culture.

- **Opening up:** Have deeper participation in supranational power structures and more international cooperation.

- **Sharing:** Encourage the people of China to share the fruits of economic growth to bridge the existing welfare gaps.

For more than thirty years—up until 2015—China was the world's fastest-growing major economy. With growth rates long running over 10 percent per annum, it has become the world's second-largest economy by nominal GDP and the world's largest economy by purchasing power parity, according to the International Monetary Fund (IMF).[48] Having such a large economy makes it difficult to achieve high growth rates. On a per capita basis, China still has a long way to develop. IMF figures[49] rank China seventieth in nominal GDP per capita ranking, valued at US$8,113. The United States ranked seventh with a value

---

48 "IMF Data," *International Monetary Fund*, accessed July 10, 2017, http://www.imf. org/en/Data.

49 "IMF: World Economic Outlook (WEO) Database, April 2017," *Knoema*, accessed July 10, 2017, https://knoema.com/IMFWEO2017Apr/ imf-world-economic-outlook-weo-database-april-2017.

of $57,436, and the United Kingdom ranked nineteenth with a value of $40,096. In each of these cases, there will of course be large variances within the population. And, in the case of China, the same applies to the variation between the well-developed eastern seaboard cities of Shanghai, Beijing, Shenzhen, and other inland cities versus the rural population.

Chinese leader Xi Jinping has set Two Centenaries, or aspirations. First is the centenary of the founding of the Communist Party of China in 2021, at which point, a full *xiaokang* society would have been achieved. *Xiaokang* roughly translates to "moderately well-off," with a rough quantitative target of doubling the 2010 per capita income by 2021. The second aspiration for the centenary of the founding of the People's Republic of China is that in 2049, China will have become a "strong, democratic, civilized, harmonious, and modern socialist country."

While you can see other proclamations and question their details, I raise these examples to give a different perspective on the approach and thinking in China. You may also recognize some of these aspirations and approaches to driving innovation and change in other locations such as Singapore and Israel but on a smaller scale.

For further thoughts on this, I suggest a TED video by

Eric Li, called "A Tale of Two Political Systems."[50] In it, Li contrasts the Western political and free-market system with the Chinese system. Li's perspective on the "legitimacy," "adaptability," and "meritocracy" of the Chinese system is an interesting one.

Some have said the Chinese economy is overreliant on investments and will falter due to its lack of democracy. However, when other financial markets have crashed, China has remained steadfast. The United States is generally becoming more protectionist during these down times, looking inward, while the Chinese economy pushes forward as a growth engine.

There are three perspectives I first outlined in 2012 that describe the reasons why China has grown and continues to thrive as a hotbed of innovation.

GREAT WALL OF CHINA

Over three decades of growth, we have seen that China has been building its economy and Western companies have been selling into the growing economy. The trade in goods with China has been in China's favor. In the case of the United States, the trade deficit in goods to China has aver-

---

50 Eric X. Li, "A Tale of Two Political Systems," *TED Talks*, accessed July 10, 2017, http://www.ted.com/talks/eric_x_li_a_tale_of_two_political_systems.

aged around $330 billion per year[51] in the period from 2011 to 2016. As investment in infrastructure has been drawing in commodities, it has become more difficult to sell in Western products. I would say the Chinese economy has grown behind its "walls," and Western companies have resorted to trying to toss products into the region to sell. Instead of seeing large returns, though, they have often been met with language barriers, cultural barriers, and the Chinese economic system—which, understandably, supports the specific growth of the Chinese economy, not outsiders' economies.

There is also what has been termed the Great Firewall of China. From an Internet protection point of view, China has been successful in developing massive, innovative, and fast-growing technology businesses that are now some of the world's most valuable companies. The leading three are referred to as BAT—Baidu, Alibaba, and Tencent. Baidu is a Chinese search engine, roughly the equivalent of Google in the West. Alibaba emerged as a successful retail sales business similar to eBay and Amazon and went on to create cloud computing options for customers. It also has the leading financial services solutions in its associate business Ant Financials. Tencent originated from an online gaming business and went on to create the WeChat platform, which has grown to

---

51 United States Census Bureau, "Foreign Trade: U.S. Trade in Goods with China," accessed July 10, 2017, https://census.gov/foreign-trade/balance/c5700.html.

become a vital social media communication platform for financial transactions in retail, transportation, and other markets. Behind the Great Firewall of China, BAT built new capabilities and has seen tremendous returns as a result of those innovative efforts.

NEW SILK ROAD

Over the years, China has gone from manufacturing inexpensive items to using its manufacturing prowess to instead dominate high-level markets such as sophisticated electronics and energy. Along with plastic toys, the country is now producing solar panels and high-speed trains.

As Tim Smith of Rouse illustrated in a discussion of IP at a Henley Business School Business and Technology SIG meeting[52] about China, the region's robust capabilities have aligned to make it a powerhouse in manufacturing; he used the example of wind turbines and wind energy. In the 1990s, the government set the policy to develop the industrial capabilities with joint ventures and technology transfer. In 1997, the State Development Planning Commission (SDPC) established a requirement for 20 percent local content. In 2000, the National Development and Reform Commission (NDRC) planned ambitious wind farm projects and set 40 percent local content requirements. As a result of the

---

52 Tim Smith, Henley Business School Business & Technology SIG, February 21, 2017.

growing market, the world's major wind turbine manufacturers tapped Chinese manufacturing subsidiaries or joint ventures to meet 70 percent of those local content requirements. By 2008, there were seventy domestic wind turbine manufacturers holding over 50 percent market share of the Chinese market. In 2010, the minimum local content requirement was dropped. By 2011, four of the ten largest wind turbine manufacturers were Chinese.

China's growth model in the wind turbine market has been replicated many times in other sectors. A leading corporate we work with made early investments in alternative energy in the early 2000s. They have since divested from those endeavors, though, because the Chinese manufacturing base was too strong to compete against in terms of producing solar panels. Similarly, a consumer goods business we are working with has over 95 percent of its manufacturing for next-generation products based in China—and, also importantly, 80 percent of the patents for those products exist within the region as well. For these reasons and more, understanding the ecosystem supporting China's growth engine is critical to corporates looking to invest in and develop its global innovation.

ENTER THE DRAGON

Because of its expansive growth, China now has the

potential to expand out of the region and both create and dominate significant new markets. An example is Huawei Technologies Co., Ltd. (pronounced "Wah-Way"), a telecommunications business. Over the last decade, Huawei has moved from a telecom business similar to Cisco or Ericsson to a dominant IT technology infrastructure business, also building market share in devices such as mobile phones. Huawei has introduced its 21st Century Network in the United Kingdom, providing devices and infrastructure for telecom businesses around the world. To accomplish this task, Huawei had to both build on existing technological capabilities and expand geographically, dominating in Africa and other emerging markets. It also had to ensure its operation was scalable and able to fit into older economies. It is not as large in the United States due to the barriers being placed on national security grounds.

Huawei is not alone in its approach. Tencent's social media advancements via WeChat, for example, have allowed the company to build new capabilities and solutions around the sales side of social media while forming new relationships with consumers as well as creating entirely new business models. Jeffrey Li, managing partner of Tencent Investments, has spoken extensively at my academy program about his company's efforts in developing the ecosystem with venturing for the business of the future.[53]

---

53 Jeffrey Li, Tencent Ventures, Nov. 2016—Video Interview.

In my interview with Arvind Sodhani, who worked at Intel for thirty-five years, led Intel Capital for ten years, and had invested in more than 1,400 companies, I asked about Intel and China.

Sodhani: We started investing in China in 1998, and we were one of the first VC investors to arrive in China. Over the years, we invested over half a billion dollars in VC start-up companies. Initially, we started investing in companies to create a total available market (TAM) expansion in those countries—that is, endeavors like getting portals up and running by companies like sohu.com, using software geared toward the Chinese language. That was just to get the PC market going in China.

Over the years, we have continued to invest in what I would call business model innovation in the sense that every country has their unique way of doing business, and you need applications that will address their business practices. For example, banking and insurance tend to be very unique to each country and each market, so you cannot take a banking or an insurance application from another country. We invested in many of those.

Now, increasingly in China, we are beginning to see technology innovations that are unique and relevant. A key facet to the Chinese marketplace is that the core structure of Chinese manufacturing and the income levels in China dictate that products must meet a much lower cost than in other parts of the world. Products, then, must be able to meet the price points that make sense in China; you simply cannot take products that are in the mainstream. You cannot take products that sell in the US or in Europe and sell them in China. If you did, you'd get the top-tier consumers with that product, but you'd never get the mainstream, high-volume consumers because the price points are much lower.

Gaule: I have seen in the past in China, and written about, what I would term "enter the dragon": that we're going to see technologies and business models rising within China, which will then come out. Are you seeing leading technologies or business models that are now going to become global rather than just being local to China?

Sodhani: Yes, we're already seeing that. For example, the China technology ecosystem that develops the tablets and smartphones is exporting tablets and smartphones to countries all over the world. India is one of their biggest overseas markets. Indonesia and Africa are also large, growing markets. We are seeing the ability of those manufacturers to be able to address global markets with innovation that started in China.

KEY MESSAGES

Technology, innovation, and start-ups are global, and there are now global centers that are growing new technologies and business models. We have only briefly looked at some examples, as the specifics depend on the technology, industry, and market—all of which vary in relevance from organization to organization. I provided my perspective on China, as it is a case for growing technology, new manufacturing capabilities, and rapidly expanding markets. It also has aspiring entrepreneurs who could drive what I have termed "Enter the Dragon."

Jack Ma, the charismatic founder of Alibaba, has a vision in which his company is viable for one hundred years. To get there, he has clear foresight about how technologies will affect many industries, not just his own—health, entertainment, retail, finance, and more. Ma knows that the new strategies coming out of China and other global superpowers could be at the forefront of creating the business models of the future.

The key point is that corporates must consider corporate venturing in start-ups in innovation hotbeds located around the globe, far from their head office. Why? For corporates endeavoring to produce Innovative New Value Chains, understanding the global markets is a key step. Linking with China to understand what is happening in terms of technology, for example, is as crucial as linking with Russia to understand advancements in physics and Israel to understand new developments in data security.

10. USING ANALYTICS TO DRIVE STRATEGIC INNOVATION AND CVC

Do feel free to share!
@agaule

We have looked at the purpose for strategic innovation and corporate venturing. Now, understanding what is happening in the investment in technology with key investors, cross sectors, and geographies is key to joining the Innovative New Value Chains. Guided data analysis can help corporates choose investments that will best support their strategies and positively impact their bottom lines. A source of this data is Global Corporate Venturing and its GCV Analytics, providing big-picture insight into corporate investments as well as granular data to include deals made by industry and sector.[54] Other useful data sources include CB Insights, Pitchbook, Silicon Valley Bank SVB Analytics, Zero2IPO, and others, which each have their own uses, regional data, and areas of expertise.

Before exploring the data, it is imperative to note that the data shown in this chapter is only a snapshot of what is happening in the corporate venturing community in terms of direct investment, as opposed to partnering or any of the other strategies discussed in previous chapters. This represents the tip of the iceberg in corporate venturing activities. Being involved in the corporate venturing ecosystem means understanding the backstories behind the data—the provisions and actions that preceded or will likely follow these direct investments.

HOW OTHER CORPORATES ARE APPROACHING CORPORATE VENTURING

As shown in figure 8, the number of corporate venturing deals around the globe has increased from 813 in 2011 to 2,018 in 2016. The size of the deals in total—not necessarily the amount each corporate has invested but the

---

54 Source and up to date data can be accessed at www.gcvanalytics.com

sum of those activities—increased from $77 billion in 2015 to $84 billion in 2016. It is also important to note the different sectors in which organizations are choosing to make minority stake investments. IT, as expected, is one of the largest, and health, finance, and media are also important. The transport sector, which has included investments in the likes of ride-sharing businesses such as Uber and DiDi (the Chinese equivalent of Uber), have been significant players as well.

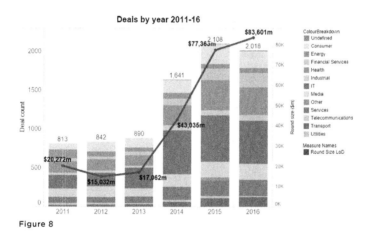

Figure 8

While the data in figure 8 is indeed telling, there are outliers to consider as well. A significant factor in the years 2015 and 2016, for example, was the heightened number of mega-investments in transport. When reviewing the data, it's important to understand that corporates don't make all their transactions public (or sometimes announce them long after an investment date has passed).

The purpose of analyzing data points is to gather insight that shows where particular industries are headed as well as where the market for corporate venturing is headed. I have been involved in corporate venturing since 2000, and I have seen corporate venturing go through cycles. When the dot-com bubble burst, for instance, many individual investors and entire corporates fell out of the market. Over the last seventeen years, though, the number of corporates as well as their longevity in the market has continued to grow, irrespective of the peaks and troughs in the cycle.

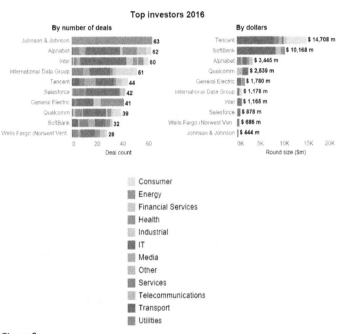

Figure 9

Figure 9 shows the top investors of 2016. Johnson & Johnson led overall and within the health sector. Alphabet, Google's parent company, followed, and Intel came third on the list. In terms of the number of deals, there is clearly a mixture of organizations participating. In terms of value, though, it is clear that Chinese corporates—likely due to the scale of the current market in China—are involved in larger deals rather than larger quantities of investments.

Once the annual baseline data is established, it is possible to drill down to gain more granular insights. For example, Ant Financial, an affiliate company of the Alibaba Group, invested in one of the biggest deals, ride-sharing company DiDi Chuxing, and in this data we can see the deal size, not the amount invested.

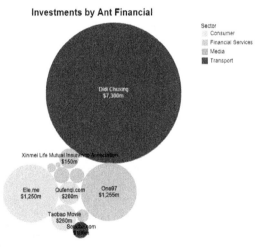

Figure 10

The international aspect of the CVC and VC funds is an important aspect for corporates, especially when considering the global nature of joining tech and start-ups and creating Innovative New Value Chains. With respect to China, over just a few years it has gone from a model that was previously offshore—for example, the Cayman Island fund investment into China—to the growth of local capabilities and funds, to current local domestic funding, as is shown in figures 11 and 12. The ability to invest in local Renminbi (RMB) currency (and being able to then repatriate funds) is now becoming more of a challenge for organizations outside of China. Chinese corporates and funds are now also making significant investments and acquisitions of intellectual property and start-ups as they build their capabilities and Innovative New Value Chains. We are seeing the data validate the "Enter the Dragon" scenario as Chinese corporates can come to dominate some new markets.

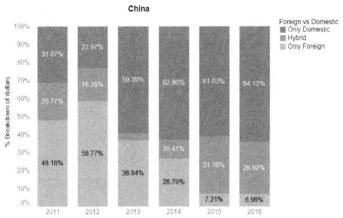

Figure 11

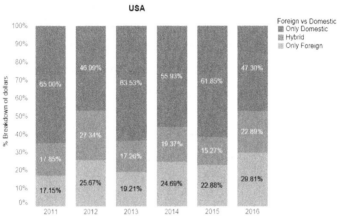

Figure 12

PARTNERING FOR INVESTING

Those interested in corporate venturing can use data to examine samples of corporate venturing players today and how they spread their investments across sectors. It is obvious from the data points shown in figures 11 and 12, coupled with the list of top investors shown in figure 9, that corporates successful in the world of corporate venturing think outside their current market.

The data shows top trends and key players in the world of corporate venturing, and it also shows the moves those key players are making in terms of joining forces with other companies and investing in sectors outside their main business models. For example, Comcast, a media business, has invested in services, media, IT, financial services, and consumer goods. Intel has predictably invested in IT services, but it has also invested in health and energy. Alibaba and Tencent, online companies in China, have invested heavily into the transport sector via a carpooling business.

Figure 13

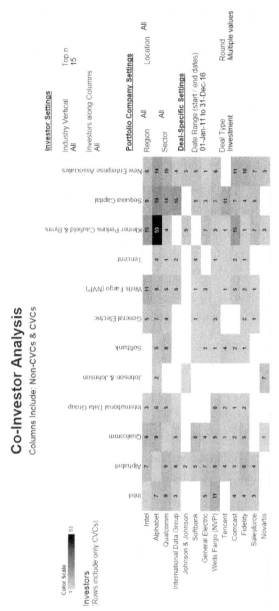

Co-Investor Analysis
Columns Include: Non-CVCs & CVCs

Companies are even investing alongside competitors and collaborators in some areas. For example, Intel has invested alongside Alphabet and Qualcomm, key competitors in the technology ecosystem. Both Qualcomm and Intel produce chips, but the data shows they invested in nine deals *together* between 2011 and 2016. They have also made deals with Kleiner Perkins Caufield & Byers and Sequoia, other venture capital firms and CVCs. These and other organizations share a common commitment to move their respective industries forward via a unifying dedication to technology and innovation.

INSIGHTS FROM EXAMINING THE DATA

When organizations are considering start-ups, deals, and data, they need to review the changing landscape for technology, start-ups, and investors. There will be many funds, start-ups, and ecosystems to keep track of. This is just a selection of companies that have raised funding in the smart home space. As we can see in figure 14,[55] there are many different approaches, devices, and technologies that are addressing solutions in the home. These will be integrated with other solutions, such as mobile infrastructure, cloud computing, big data, artificial intelligence, new

---

55 "Smart Home Market Map: 60 Startups in Home Automation, Smart Appliances, and More," *CB Insights* (blog), July 10, 2017, www.cbinsights.com/blog/smart-home-market-map-company-list/.

social media interaction, payment, and value capture for the participant companies.

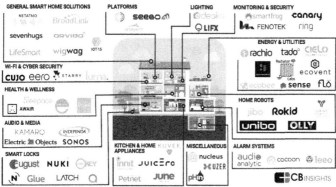

Figure 14

These ecosystems will be repeated for health, automotive, industrial, technology, and more. The challenge for organizations and CVCs is keeping track, identifying the key start-ups at the right time, and engaging to invest and collaborate to orchestrate Innovative New Value Chains. Being involved in the deal flow and ecosystem will help them recognize where they can add and capture value.

KEY MESSAGES

Strategic innovation and venturing is a global task. Organizations will need to view data to see where deals are being done, where investments are being made, and potentially how they can be connected. Reviewing external data and connecting the internal processes, people, and performance measures will be important to help to define and align the strategic purpose.

MOVING FORWARD

Over the course of this book, we have gone on a journey, examining how corporates need to think about strategically aligning innovation and venturing to create Innovative New Value Chains instead of adhering to the status quo and making ad hoc investments. We have noted that failure to embrace Innovative New Value Chains will not necessarily lead to business failure—aka a "Kodak moment"—but it *can* lead to missed opportunities worth billions of dollars. We've covered how stringing together different start-ups and technologies to create new value propositions for customers is how to get out in front of disruption in a given industry. So, what is the next step?

Going forward, C-suite executives, corporate venturing teams, and others participating in innovation need to have strategic discussions about the future of not only the business but also the global market—a discussion critical to the viability of the business in the long term.

That conversation, though, cannot be had in abstract terms. The 5Ps—purpose, process, people, partners, and performance—come into play here to build the foundation for strategic innovation and context for Innovative New Value Chains.

As I've worked with C-suite and board-level clients over the years, many have turned to me and said the discussion of the 5Ps was the first time they had had a proper strategy discussion in a long time, if ever. Why? Many corporates focus too heavily on new product launches, mergers with and acquisitions of sector competitors, or R&D rather than looking ahead to the future of their industry. Examples include oil companies losing market share to alternative-energy organizations, tobacco companies being challenged by the vaping industry, banks grappling with social media payments, and car companies losing ground to autonomous electric vehicle sharing.

To avoid disruption, corporates must focus on bringing processes together in a way that is both agile and iterative. The critical process of realigning strategy is ongoing and influenced by the world of technologies and expanding business models. Those who excel in corporate venturing know how to turn that perspective into action, bringing insights home to the central decision-making organization (or, as I've described, the hive). When it is time to create a new hive or business model, then, those corporates will be ready to make that significant change.

As shown in the wealth of data in chapter ten, corporates are investing so much in sectors outside their respective industries that entirely new business models and ecosystems are being created as a result. In fact, the corporate venturing ecosystem is buzzing such that entire industries are being reframed—industries such as automotive, health, consumer goods, and IT are all in the process of constant evolution because they are seeing such a high level of convergence.

Developing Innovative New Value Chains and participating in corporate venturing are worth the effort because successful organizations can partner in ways that are not only profitable but also make the world a better place, making significant improvements in health, sustainability, and other areas that are improving the lives of people around the globe.

ACKNOWLEDGMENTS

I'd like to acknowledge the support of the corporate venturing and innovation ecosystem and Global Corporate Venturing, an organization at the center of this community. Thank you to the corporate venture capital leaders and senior executives within the corporate landscape who have supported me in the development of this thinking through their discussions, interviews, videos, and friendship over many years. I'd also like to acknowledge my clients who continue this journey with me as they strive to complete and expand upon profitable Innovative New Value Chains.

I would also like to thank the individuals and organizations that supported the book and programs by purchasing items on the Kickstarter campaign.

In addition, I'd like to acknowledge my colleagues Gary Marsh and Debbie Rose for their input in the development of the approaches and reviews, as well as editors and publishers Barbara Boyd, Kathleen Pedersen, Jessica Burdg, and other various team members for making this possible.

SOURCES OF FURTHER INFORMATION

The resources supporting this book can be found via links at aimava.com/resources. If you have any questions or would like further information, contact Andrew Gaule (andrew.gaule@aimava.com). Subscribe to the podcasts at www.gaulesqt.podomatic.com.

GLOSSARY

A glossary of corporate venturing, venture capital, and other terms is available at aimava.com/resources.

PODCAST INTERVIEWS

FIRST NAME	LAST NAME	ORGANIZATION	MONTH/YEAR
Abdul	Guefor	Intel	Feb-12
Alex	Steel	Syngenta	Apr-13
Alexei	Levene	iXInnovation—India	Oct-14
Andrew	Gaule	China markets	Nov-10

FIRST NAME	LAST NAME	ORGANIZATION	MONTH/YEAR
Arvind	Sadhani	Intel Capital	Mar-15
Ben	Luckett	Aviva	Mar-16
Bernhard	Mohr	Evonik Venture Capital and CIO	Oct-13
Bill	Taranto	Merck Global Health Innovation	Apr-17
Bill	Taranto	Merck	May-11
Bob	Ackerman	Allegis Capital	Dec-10
Brad	Vale	J & J Ventures	Jan-14
Brian	Lowry	Caterpillar Ventures	Sep-16
Bruce	Beckloff	ARM	Nov-11
Chris	Wade	UKTI VC Unit	Sep-13
Claudia	Fan	IBM Venture Capital Group	Sep-14
Claus	Schmidt	Bosch	Nov-12
Curt	Hopkins	Alacrity Foundation	Mar-14
David	Atkinson	Tate & Lyle	Mar-13
David	Roth	Entrepreneur with corporate	Feb-13
David	Phillips	SR One	Mar-12
Debbie	Brackeen	Citi Ventures	Aug-13
Dominique	Mégret	Swisscom	Jun-12
Eric	Steager	Independence Blue Cross	Sep-15
Frank	Lampen	Distill Ventures	Oct-15
Frank	Herkstroter	P&G	Dec-11
Geoff	McGrath	McLaren	Apr-15
Geoff	McGrath	McLaren	Aug-10
Gerald	Brady	Silicon Valley Bank	Dec-14

FIRST NAME	LAST NAME	ORGANIZATION	MONTH/YEAR
Gert	van de Wouw	Shell Technology Ventures	Dec-13
Girish	Nadkarni	ABB	Dec-12
Graeme	Martin	Takeda	Oct-11
Gwen	Melincoff	Shire Strategic Investment Group	Aug-12
Harshul	Sanghi	American Express Ventures	Jul-15
Iain	Bomphray	Williams Advanced Engineering	Mar-17
Iain	Cooper	Schlumberger	May-13
Ignaas	Caryn	KLM and Mainport Ventures	Jan-15
Jacqueline	LeSage Krause	Munich Re/ Hartford Steam Boiler	Jan-16
Jay	Reinmann	Managing Partner of Propel, BBVA Bank CVC	May-16
Jelto	Smits	Prime Technology Ventures	Oct-10
Jeremy	Basset	Unilever Foundry	Jun-15
John	Hamer	Monsanto	Apr-14
John	Suh	Hyundai Ventures	Nov-13
Jon	Lauckner	GM Ventures	May-15
Jon	Hague	Unilever	May-12
Jörg	Sievert	SAP Ventures	Jul-11
Josef	Wünsch	BASF	Sep-11

FIRST NAME	LAST NAME	ORGANIZATION	MONTH/YEAR
Justin	Adams	BP	Jan-11
Kemal	Anbarci	Chevron	Feb-15
Laurel	Buckner	MD GCI Ventures	Jun-16
Marcel	Lubben	DSM	Apr-12
Marek	Rubasinski	Sky Ventures	Jun-17
Martin	Kelly	IBM and Smart Camp	Jul-12
Martin	Grieve	Unilever	Jun-11
Matthew	Koertge	Telstra Ventures	Feb-17
Mehmood	Kahn	PepsiCo	Dec-16
Michael	Blaustein	DuPont Ventures Chair of CVG at NVCA	Nov-14
Mike	Weeks	Wells Fargo	Aug-14
Miles	Adcock	QinetiQ	Jun-13
Miles	Kirby	Qualcomm	Jan-13
Nagraj	Kashyap	Microsoft Ventures	Oct-16
Naomi	Fried	CIO Boston Children's Hospital	May-14
Neil	Pennington	RWE nPower	Dec-15
Paul	Morris	Corporate Venturing Unit UKTI	Feb-16
Paul	Morris	Dow Venture Capital	Feb-11
Peter	Cowley	Martlet	Nov-15
Peter	Holliday	GSK	Oct-12
Phil	Smith	Cisco	Apr-16
Reese	Schroder	Motorola	Jan-12

FIRST NAME	LAST NAME	ORGANIZATION	MONTH/YEAR
Richard	Hughes	University and Industry interaction in Global University Venturing	Feb-14
Rob	van Leen	DSM	May-17
Rob	van Leen	DSM	Apr-12
Roel	Bulthuis	Merck MS Ventures	Jul-16
Roy	Williamson	Castrol innoVentures	Jul-13
Sridhar	Solur	HP ePrint Solutions	Sep-10
Stephen	Socolof	NVP (Secondary) and NVCA (USA VC Market)	Sep-12
Stephen	Lake	Cody Gate Ventures	Mar-11
Sue	Siegel	GE Ventures	Jun-14
Thomas	Andrae	3M New Ventures	Jul-14
Tony	Askew	Reed Elsevier	Sep-13
Ulrich	Quay	BMW	Jan-17
Vitaly	Golomb	HP Tech Ventures	Jul-17
Wendy	Lung	IBM	Apr-11
Will	Rosenzweig	Physic Ventures with Unilever	May-12
Zack	Weisfeld	Microsoft Accelerator	Nov-16

VIDEO INTERVIEWS

FIRST NAME	LAST NAME	ORGANIZATION	MONTH/YEAR
Alexander	Gornyi	MailRu	Sep-16
Cha	Li	iStart	Sep-15
Claudia	Fan Munce	IBM	May-15
David	Mayhew	GE	May-15
Dominique	Mégret	Swisscom	Jul-16
Ekaterina	Vainberg		Sep-16
Eric	Steager	Independence Blue Cross	Jan-16
Girish	Nadkarni	ABB	May-15
Harshul	Sanghi	American Express Ventures	Nov-15
Howard	Palmer	Taylor Wessing	Jun-15
Ignaas	Caryn	KLM and Mainport Ventures	Jul-15
Jan	Harley	Unilever Ventures	Jan-17
Jeffrey	Li	Tencent Ventures	Nov-16
John	Kearon	BrainJuicer	Nov-16
Jonathan	Tudor	BP Castrol	May-15
Mark	Radcliffe	DLA Piper	Jul-15
Mark	Muth	PWC	May-15
Matt	McElhattan	Chevron Technology Ventures	May-15
Paul	Morris	UKTI	May-15
Tim	Smith	Rouse	Nov-16
Tony	Askew	REV Venture Partners	Jul-16
Vadim	Konyushkevich	Liniya Prava	Sep-16
Vartan	Minasyan	Kaspersky Lab	Sep-16
Xuan	Chen	ARM	Nov-16

The resources supporting this book can be found via links at aimava.com/resources.

ABOUT THE AUTHOR

 **ANDREW GAULE** is an expert in the world of strategic innovation and corporate venturing. As the CEO of Aimava, he has helped global organizations drive innovative and strategic change. He has been leading Strategic Innovation and Corporate Venturing programs for corporates in the United States, Europe, Russia and Asia. Andrew is also an angel investor and shares his passion for innovation and entrepreneurship with young people in his UpStarts4StartUps program. He is the author of numerous reports and of the book *Open Innovation in Action*. Husband and proud father of two daughters.